I dared to live

I dared to live

by Sandra Brand

Fourth Revised, Enlarged, and Illustrated Edition

SHENGOLD BOOKS
Rockville, MD

Library of Congress Cataloging-in-Publication Data

Brand, Sandra.
I dared to live / by Sandra Brand.-- 4th rev. and expanded ed.
p.   cm.
ISBN 1-887563-50-4 -- ISBN 1-887563-49-0 (pbk.)
1. Brand, Sandra. 2. Jews--Poland--Biography. 3. Holocaust, Jewish (1939-1945)--Poland--Personal   narratives.   4.   World   War,   1939-1945--Poland--Personal narratives, Jewish. 5. Poland--Biography. I. Title.

D5135.P63 B72 2000
940.53'18'092--dc21
[B]
                                                                99-089438

To her co-workers at the Vinetta warehouse in Warsaw, she was Cecylia Szarek, an attractive young Polish woman surprisingly ambivalent toward the handsome German officer so clearly in love with her.

To the Jews trapped inside the Warsaw Ghetto, she was the "goldene shikse," a Gentile woman blessedly willing to take messages out of the ghetto and help smuggle cash inside.

Only a few trusted friends knew that "Cecylia Szarek" had been born from the ashes of a burned armband identifying her as a Jew and was kept alive by false identification papers...that behind her smiling, vivacious demeanor was the frightened daughter of a pious Hasidic family, a wife and mother desperate for news of her husband and child.

Few people were what they seemed in wartime Warsaw — Berler, the warehouse manager who entertained guests at Christmas dinner but kept a Torah hidden in his attic; little Andrzej, who prayed to Jesus but undressed in secret, lest strangers see his circumcision; Schone, who tried to hide his Semitic nose under the handkerchief of the perpetual hay fever sufferer.

Ironically, Cecylia's greatest support came from Rolf Rechter, the German officer increasingly disillusioned with the Hitler regime and willing to risk his own life to help Cecylia and her people survive. I DARED TO LIVE is a story of love and deception, intrigue and adventure, faith and despair. It is the kind of story novels are made of — but it happens to be true.

SANDRA BRAND is the author of *Between Two Worlds*. Born in Vienna, she was brought to Poland as a child and has lived in the United States since 1947. She is married to Arik Weintraub and they live in New York. Sandra Brand has lectured widely on the Holocaust.

My heartfelt thanks to

Prof. Nechama Tec, writer
Luna Tarla, writer
Dr. Richard White, editor

for their help in preparing this fourth edition

INTRODUCTION

Publishing a new edition of this heartbreaking yet also heartwarming book is a reason to celebrate. A trickle of books by those who survived the destruction of the Jews of Europe started to appear shortly after the end of World War Two. In recent years, that trickel has turned into a flood. The few thousands who had survived the death of the millions were reaching their twilight years, and the overwhelming need to bear witness — to let the world know what human beings are capable of doing to other human beings — gave rise to a library of thousands of books, most of them personal memoirs. Together, the books in this library preserve the memory of the greatest tragedy the world has ever known.

In writing about the Eichmann trial, Hannah Arendt coined the phrase "the banality of evil." Unfortunately, after you read several Holocaust memoirs, they begin to blend together, and evil becomes worn out with repetition. But what had set Sandra Brand's book apart when it was first published twenty years ago, was the fact that it was only about great evil, but also about the human capacity for good in the midst of such evil. Indeed, a great love story.

One of the readers who noticed this difference was former Israeli Attorney General Gideon Hausner, who served as state prosecutor at the Eichmann trial. Hausner wrote, "It is a remarkable book which I read almost spellbound, without putting it down. Mrs. Brand is blessed with an extraordinary gift of narration; her memory is amazing. The events which she had lived through are so different from the usual experiences of survivors and hence of special interest."

What is so different about this book is that while some 500,000 Jews were being brutalized inside the Warsaw Ghetto and systematically annihilated, a young and beautiful blond, blue-eyed Jewish girl from a hasidic family was working in a Polish factory outside the walls of the ghetto, where she had assumed the identity of a Catholic Polish woman, and became part of an underground network of people, including disguised Jews, Poles, and even a German police officer engaged in anti-Nazi activities. Each of these people was taking a heroic stand against the ultimate evil of the Nazi occupiers of Poland, resisting dehumanization, death and destruction against all odds, and prevailing in the end.

It is no wonder that over the years this book came out in three editions, and has found its way to the hearts and minds of readers in other languages, including Hebrew, Polish, and German. It was even made into a television program in Poland, and U.S. movie-makers have shown interest in turning it into a motion picture.

The new post-Holocaust generations, especially the children of both the victims and the victimizers, are looking for ways to turn a new page in our human coexistence on this small planet. In this search, Sandra Brand's story provides a ray of light in the great darkness that had fallen across Europe and continues to cast its shadow into the new millennium. It is important to know that there were good Germans, good Poles, and good Jews during the worst of times and in the worst of places. They are the ones who, according to the teachings of Judaism, save the world. They are the righteous few, thanks to whom the world continues to exist.

As this new, expanded and updated edition shows, Sandra Brand's mission to pursue and implement the positive lessons of the Holocaust has continued to this day, when she is well into her eighties. She has spent years of hard work, a great deal of money, and much of her writing talent to help those who had helped her and her fellow Jews, to pay proper tribute and to create a lasting memorial to the righteous gentiles who continue to provide hope for a better world.

The original publisher, Moshe Sheinbaum, and I, the new publisher, feel proud and privileged to offer this book once again to a new generation of readers.

Mordecai Schreiber

1

On entering the deserted lobby of a shabby apartment building on Kopernica Street in Lvov on a dreary afternoon in the year of 1941, I gripped the white armband bearing the blue star of David, pulled it off my sleeve, and stuffed it into my large pigskin handbag. I took if off with the intention of never wearing it again. Then I decided to wait a little so that the passersby who might have seen me enter would now be far away.

A change was taking place within me. With the removal of the armband which the German Occupational Authorities had ordered me to put on four months ago, I was shedding my meekness and timidity. I stood shivering in the dimly lit alcove for a few moments and then walked out into the street.

My name was no longer Roma Brand. From now on it was Cecylia Szarek.

Would I remember to answer to my new name? Was I doing the right thing in taking on this false identity and leaving everyone dear to me behind?

I had no more time to think about it because I had to meet my friend Fischer who had offered to take me by car to Warsaw where I hoped I would be safer from detection.

The Opel (a German-made small car) was waiting at the corner of Legionov Street. My friend Fischer was sitting next to the driver and Danka Bracka in the back. I got in beside her. I trusted Danka because, although she was Catholic, she had confided to me that she was going to Warsaw to try to help her Jewish fiancé who had been confined to the Ghetto.

As we left Lvov, twilight was fading into darkness and the air was damp and cold.

I began to think of Bruno, my only child, whom I'd left in the care of his father in Zloczov, not far from Lvov. I was determined to find a Polish woman in Warsaw who would board a five-year-old boy.

All at once, in the silence, I sensed Fischer had turned to look at me, but it was already too dark to decipher the expression on his face. However, I had the impression that he was smiling encouragingly.

We were approaching Rava-Ruska. Fischer had thought it unwise to stop in Rava-Ruska but I wanted to say good-bye to my oldest sister, and he had given in to my pleas.

The town looked peaceful in the dark. Fischer made the driver stop the car on a side street. I hurried across the Market Place to Anna's two-story house and knocked at the glass paneled entrance door.

"Who's there?" Anna's voice sounded apprehensive.

It was always the woman who went to the door since she was less likely to be arrested than man.

I heard footfalls in the street and quickly stepped aside so as not to stand in the light falling through the glass panels.

"Who's there?" Anna repeated.

I waited until the footfalls receded. "It's Roma, open up!"

Anna's delicate face reflected her happiness upon seeing me. I told her I could stay only for a minute and she called to her husband, Hersh, that he could now come out of hiding. She asked me for the whereabouts of my little boy and I told her, both of my plan for Bruno and that, once I was settled in Warsaw, my husband, Mark, also planned to start life under an assumed name. Of course our small family unit of three would have to split up so that if one were arrested the other might survive.

My brother-in-law nodded in agreement.

"What does Father say about all this?" I asked. I knew that in my father's eyes, it would look as though I were deserting my people. "What does Father say?" I repeated my question.

"He approves," Hersh said with a smile.

"He does?" I had wondered if my father, a deeply pious Jew, and a Belzer Hassid, who had lived all his life only for his faith would be able to understand.

"I wish more of us had your courage." Although there was no one in the house besides myself and Anna, Hersh glanced over his shoulder and lowered his voice: "I saw your father last week and he told me he would pray for you three times a day. So will your brother and I."

We embraced.

I fumbled in my bag for the armband and thrust it into Anna's hand. "Burn it," I said.

Outside, I was suddenly afraid that the car might not be there and I started to run across the Square.

The car was there. Fischer hurried to open the door for me pressing my hand in the dark.

2

Six weeks later, I was on the train from Warsaw back to Lvov. Since I could not go to Zloczov because too many people would recognize me there, I had arranged with Mark in advance that when he received a telegram from Lvov he would immediately bring Bruno to the real Cecylia Szarek, who had given her identity papers to me.

The "Cecylia Szarek" now traveling to Lvov not only had her friend's birth and baptismal certificates but also a paper stating that Warsaw was her residence and that she was employed as interpreter at the Vinetta warehouse whose proprietor, Berler, a German civilian, spoke no Polish although he had sixteen Poles in his employ.

To justify my trip, I had promised my boss to get some orders.

In Lvov the real Cecylia Szarek welcomed me heartily. She went at once to the post office to send a telegram to Mark and I went to the Promtorg building where Fischer placed a substantial order with my company. The news that he would frequently be coming to Warsaw and the big order for Vinetta put me in a happy frame of mind. I left Fischer and with brisk strides walked to my next business appointment.

"*Pani* (Mrs.) Roma, *Pani* Roma!" a man's voice startled me.

"My name is Cecylia Szarek," I said.

It was Ivan, a non-Jew from Niemirov, my home town. Caught! I had been discovered without my armband!

My face must have revealed my despair because Ivan's first words after he caught up with me were, "Don't worry, *Pani* Roma, I am your friend."

Although his tone sounded reassuring, I trembled. So many stories had been told of old neighbors denouncing Jews to the authorities that I was eager to get away from him as quickly as possible without showing that I was afraid. "Have you seen my father lately?" I asked.

"Yesterday. Yesterday I saw him in Niemirov. I came here on business this morning and am going back tomorrow. Your father is fine and so is your family. How about you, how are things with you?"

Since my right arm was without the telltale band, what could I tell him? "Forgive me, Mr. Trusievicz, I am late for an appointment. Please, give my regards to my father. And please, Mr. Trusievicz, don't tell anyone else that you have seen me." I touched his wrist. "Can you promise?"

He nodded.

"Thank you, thank you a thousand times, Mr. Trusievicz . . ."

He had been Ivan to me since we had known each other, why was I addressing him now as Mr. Trusievicz?

I rushed away feeling guilty about my suspicions of a decent man.

Hiding under my hat, my coat collar turned up, I stole to my next appointment.

I expected Mark and Bruno to arrive the following day or the day after. When they did not come, I sent another telegram and got an answer: "Dr. Mark Rathauser and family have moved out." The telegram was signed by the *Judenrat* (authority of the Jewish community created by the Germans to also serve as an intermediary with the Germans). I could not understand why, if my husband had moved, he had not left a forwarding address. And what about his parents and sister who also lived with him? Perhaps it was his sister's idea for she was against letting Bruno go to Warsaw with me in the first place. I wanted to ask Fischer for advice but was stopped from doing this by the curfew.

My wedding had taken place in 1936, in Lvov, in the two-room apartment of a poverty-stricken rabbi, who for twenty-five zlotys, had agreed to perform the ceremony without the special parental permit required for minors under the age of eighteen. In the center of a room with ancient cabinets, bookcases, scratched tables and

*broken chairs jammed against the peeling walls giving the whole
decor the appearance of a warehouse, stood the wedding canopy.*

*There were two witnesses, in addition to whom the rabbi had
supplied ten men (the required minyan) to recite the prayers.
Neither Mark's parents nor mine were present during the
ceremony. Both our families were against the marriage so we
eloped. My father refused to give us his blessing because Mark was
totally assimilated and twice my age, whereas Mark's family
wanted their spoilt darling to marry money. Even after the birth of
our son a year later, there still was friction between the two
families.*

First thing in the morning I showed Fischer the telegram.
"What does it mean?" I cried. "In this case I'll go to Zloczov and
fetch Bruno. If Mark wants to come along, all right. If not —"

"You can't go to Zloczov . . ." He didn't look at me.

"Zloczov is a small town, I'll find them. Besides, the *Judenrat*
must know where they're staying."

Now he looked at me. "Cecylia, if the telegram had read *UM-
gesiedelt* there would be hope that Mark had voluntarily changed
his living quarters. But *AUS-gesiedelt* implies something completely different."

"Deportation?" I took a deep breath.

"These things happen so quickly," he said and took my hand.
"It's senseless to go. Besides, there is an *Action* on in Zloczov right
now. You couldn't help them." He hesitated, "And it could be
fatal for you."

I went straight to the railroad station and three hours later arrived in Zloczov.

The area was deserted. But on Mickievicza Street where my
in-laws used to live I saw, walking in pairs in my direction under
the custody of armed guards, about thirty men and women with
armbands on their sleeves. I wanted desperately to find out
whether there was anyone I knew but "Cecylia Szarek" restrained
me.

What if someone called out to me? 'Don't go to Zloczov,' I
heard Fischer say. 'It could be fatal for you . . . Fatal . . .'

After the column had shuffled past, a larger group appeared.
The *Action* Fischer had mentioned was in full swing. I bent my
head and not looking to my right nor to my left, I raced back to the

railroad station. I didn't inquire at the *Judenrat*. I didn't ask for my in-laws' new address.

On the way a woman's voice called, *"Pani mecenasova* (Mrs. Attorney), *Pani mecenasova."*

I looked up. It was a Polish neighbor of my in-laws. I waved back to her but when the thought struck me that she, unlike Ivan, might report me for the crime of not wearing the telltale armband, I ran off.

For three hours the wheels of the train taking me back to Lvov hummed: "I have something important to tell you *Pani mecenasova*, something important . . ."

3

Back in Warsaw, without Bruno, without Mark, I had to go to work as usual.

On Mazoviecka Street, I passed the antique shop of Mrs. Lesnievska who owned the building in which the Vinetta offices were located. The creaking door, the dark hall, the worn stairs up to the second floor landing, and the heavy doors at both ends of the windowless corridor all contributed to a generally threatening atmosphere.

The employees entered through the door on the right. Only Berler, the boss, had a key to the door on the left.

Since the fifteen other clerks at their desks in the large main office were sitting with their backs to me, I was able to slip into my cubicle unnoticed. I hung up my coat, touched up my hair and entered Berler's office to report the orders I had secured in Lvov.

Berler rewarded me for the orders I had netted his company by putting me in charge of checking the merchandise manufactured by Ghetto inhabitants.

My telephone rang constantly and there were always clients lined up at my desk. Any doubts I had had about my ability to cope with Berler were dismissed immediately.

My assignment to deal with BBH, the Jewish manufacturing firm in the Ghetto, provided me with an ideal means of contact with my people. Berler instructed me as to how to comply with the established procedures laid down by the *Transferstelle,* the official intermediary between the Ghetto and the Aryan side of the city. It was there one obtained a pass to the Ghetto and a permit for the transfer of BBH products to the Vinetta warehouse on the Aryan side.

My new duties gave me the opportunity to speak to the BBH manager when he came to the Vinetta offices for conferences with Berler. We also spoke over the phone. He was the only Jew I met in Warsaw but he never learned that I was one. At times my courteous manner to him would change radically in the middle of a conversation because somebody had entered my cubicle. However, my actions revealed unequivocally that I was on his side.

From Vinetta BBH procured German work cards for its employees that they cherished more than their salaries because, at that time, these documents provided some immunity from raids and entitled their recipients to additional food coupons.

The manager of BBH called on me for both trivial and important matters. Often he asked for work cards for "Employees" whom I knew did not work at BBH. At other times he made a personal request for a pass to the Aryan side of the city on behalf of a member of what appeared to be a suspiciously large family.

When he wanted anything as, for example, quicker payments, a message conveyed to someone outside the Ghetto, a good word put in for him to Berler, or an excuse for his company's unavoidable delay in finishing an order, he also turned to me for help.

With or without Fischer's advice, I was able to solve most of these problems.

It was difficult for a non-Jew to get into the Ghetto as it was for a Jew to get out. Since a petitioner applying for a pass in the *Transferstelle* had to answer innumerable questions, and received a permit only in rare cases, few people even applied.

I longed for information about life inside the Ghetto, but was afraid that even by only listening to gossip about it, I would give away my emotions.

Once I referred to the manager of BBH as Mr. Korman whereupon my co-workers burst into laughter and one of them said: "Since when do you call a Jew mister?"

It took all my arts of deception to erase the impression that I was a Jewish sympathizer.

But I could not refrain from asking: "Do you really think all of them are bad? Don't you think that there are some good ones?"

"Of course," Zosia, the typist, said.

Suddenly Zosia's small deep-set eyes seemed beautiful to me. I wanted to be friends with her.

I saw little of Danka, who had come to Warsaw with me and had moved into my room at the boarding house on Hoza Street. Usually she would spend the night away from home and would not tell me where she had been. Whenever I asked her about getting her fiancé out of the Ghetto her answers were evasive. Despite the fact that I paid the rent and had helped her get a job at Vinetta and, above all, had entrusted my secret to her, she did not seem to trust me.

As long as I was busy I could keep myself from thinking. But as soon as I had a moment to myself, especially before going to bed, I was haunted by visions of men, women and children, all with armbands, shuffling past me, their eyes accusing. Worst of all I would see my Bruno among them and hear his voice calling out: 'Mummy, don't leave me. I want to go with you. Please, don't leave me.'

No, Bruno could not possibly be in that column. I had to believe that my child had not been deported. When Mark realized that a large *Action* was imminent he must have placed him with a Polish friend in Zloczov.

In the loneliness of my room I would speak aloud to my son: "Bruno, my darling, I wanted to take you with me. But Daddy insisted that you stay with him until I found a home for you. And as soon as I did, I went to get you but it was too late. I love you, my darling, and I will find you soon."

But then I would be anxious with fear. *How* would I find out with *whom* Mark had placed Bruno? It would be impossible.

After the war, I would find a way. I would have to find a way.

4

"Miss Szarek!" Berler called. "We're going to the Ghetto with a couple of customers."

The girls in the office overhearing this made their comments:
"Watch out, the Jews are dirty —"

"They have lice —"

"Keep your distance —"

"Make sure you take a bath before coming back to the office," one shouted across the other.

Zosia, with a twinkle in her eye, whispered: "You're lucky. I wish I were going."

In Warsaw of that period a trip to the Ghetto was regarded as first-class entertainment.

We arrived in a Mercedes. With me were Berler, Fischer — representing Promtorg, and Mr. Widerko — representing a Ukrainian firm. The Gestapo guard checked our permits and let us pass.

My heart was beating madly.

We entered a teaming beehive.

All along the sides of buildings ragged, emaciated creatures huddled in the sun and the moment a spot was vacated it was taken by another. At first glance they seemed to be old people; at a second look, however, I knew they were prematurely aged.

A man trotting next to our slow moving car, looked straight at me. His cracked lips moved soundlessly. Coins rattled in the tin cup tied to a rope that hung from his withered neck. His clothes had been repaired so often that one could not tell the patches from the original fabric. Special care had been given that the sleeves be decently mended to provide a background for the wearing of the armband.

Reaching for a coin, I noticed Berler watching me curiously and instead of my wallet, I drew out my handkerchief. I caught a last glimpse of the beggar's soiled open palms, and in my mind, I heard my father say, 'Never let a beggar turn away empty-handed.'

Once when I was a child, my father had asked me if I could keep a secret. I had looked up at him and said, 'Of course, I can.'

He handed me a ten zloty bill and lowered his voice to a whisper: 'Give this to Fishel or his wife and don't ever tell anyone about it!'

'But, Father, he is a horse thief.'

'A thief has to eat too,' had been his reply.

After that I became his messenger on many other similar occasions.

Now, as a liaison between the Ghetto and the world outside, perhaps I was still playing out the same childish games of secret charity I had shared with my father. Or perhaps, by having to turn my back on this beggar in order to keep up my pretense of being non-Jewish, I was also betraying him. My position was ambivalent — and I was riddled with guilt.

Fischer called my attention to posters advertising floor shows and dance music in nightclubs for those who still had the money to go. Virtuosos, who had formerly toured the biggest concert halls of Europe, now performed there for a hot meal. Many restaurants featured chamber music. Berler mentioned some places frequented by the Gestapo after work.

The many ragged people and the few elegant moved as if they had been struck by disease. Feverish eyes, enormous for the thin faces, stared at the car and then turned away. Their food allowance was a hundred-and-eighty-four calories a day.

The car stopped in front of BBH. Berler got out first and stumbled over a long package covered with sheets of newspaper. With his silver-knobbed cane he poked at it. It was a corpse.

So many died daily that the undertakers could not cope with the load.

Widerko took a long time admiring the quality of the leather

Zosia. one of the author's co-workers at Vinetta.

The author as "Cecylia Szarek" (1942)

*The real Cecylia Szarek (1941), a third generation catholic who
gave the author her birth and baptismal certificates.*

Maria Lasocka, a coworker at Vinetta. She was a Jew living as a Catholic with false papers.

pocketbooks prepared for shipping to Vinetta. Today, he tripled his order. "They produce better things than we do on the outside. Where do they get the raw material?"

I smiled at him and he continued:

"Do they bribe the guards?"

"The Germans are not corruptible," Berler said and the subject was dropped.

That evening in my rooms behind closed doors, Fischer said: "Did you see the posters advertising concerts? They're half-starved but they go to concerts . . ."

Wasn't he giving himself away by the sudden outburst of proud identification?

My friendship with Fischer had developed when both of us were working in a department store nationalized by the Russians who had occupied Lvov from 1939 until 1941. In June of that year, after chasing the Russians out of Lvov, the Germans took over the firm and fired all the Jews. Until then it had been taken for granted that Fischer was Jewish. However, afterwards he made a point of giving a different impression. He made it known that he was of the same Protestant faith as his separated wife and children. He even became a Volksdeutscher *(a Polish citizen of German descent who, after filing an application with the German Authorities could become a* second class *German). His claim seemed to be true because not only was he not fired as the Jews were, but he was actually promoted.*

I, for one, had believed him for I saw no reason that he should not be entirely open with me.

Now, when he praised the inmates of the Ghetto, some doubts took hold. No man in his right mind would do such thing. I was about to ask Fischer directly whether he was Jewish, when Danka's return interrupted our confidential conversation.

5

The boarding house on Hoza Street managed by Kasia had become my new "home." But I wanted to move when I heard Kasia say, "Hitler is an evil man but he did something good for us — he rid us of the Jewish pest." Still, I stayed on. She respected boarders recommended by Berler and would never suspect a protegé of his. She kept our rooms spotlessly clean and woke us every morning in time to go to work.

Breakfast was served in the living room which was the focal point of the house. From the living room ran the long corridor with the boarders' many doors on one side. On the opposite side there were doors to the large kitchen, the communal bathroom, Kasia's room and the landlady's quarters.

A cold winter had passed during which America had entered the war. Hope for a quick end to the fighting soon dwindled. The days became longer and the weather milder.

One evening Kasia knocked at my door. "Can you come out for a minute?" she asked. "Two gentlemen sent by Berler are here. They need a room for one night. I told them there was no vacancy, but they won't leave."

I followed Kasia into the living room and saw Widerko, the man who had praised Jewish know-how in the Ghetto, and another man I didn't know. I turned to Kasia and said that the two men had placed substantial orders with Vinetta and we should do something to accommodate them. I suggested that Kasia set them up in my room. I would sleep on one of the living-room couches and, if Danka came home for the night, she could sleep on the other as we had done before.

I took what Danka and I needed from my room and waited in the living room for the boarders to retire so that I could undress and go to bed.

I could hear the sound of water dripping from the leaking kitchen faucet. I should have closed the kitchen door but I sat in a wooden armchair too tired to move. I removed an envelope from my pigskin pocketbook, made sure I heard no footsteps, and took out Bruno's photograph.

Each time I looked at it his face came alive. The eyes became blue, the hair flaxen. I could smell the aroma of hay it exuded. Born big and healthy he had become painfully thin after a bout with the measles. "Eat my child, eat," I murmured. But is he hungry? Is he cold? Is there anyone to love him? How I longed to press him to my heart, to rub noses as we used to!

Suddenly the kitchen door slammed.

I stood up facing two German soldiers.

"You lost your way?" I asked in German.

"No," one of them said. He had a glass eye and I found his stare unnerving. "We are looking for a girl who has recently come from Lvov."

"I don't know anyone from Lvov. The landlady might know," I said.

"Where can we find her?"

Fumbling behind my back, I succeeded in pushing the photo of Bruno under my pocketbook. "There," I said, pointing into the corridor toward the landlady's door.

"Let's go, Hans," said the German with the glass eye.

As soon as they had turned their backs, I quickly put the photo into my pocketbook and slumped down on the chair. They were looking for me. I was the girl from Lvov.

I heard the landlady's door open and in a moment they were back with me.

"We need you as interpreter. Come along."

No, they had not come for me.

With the landlady leading, we proceeded toward the boarders' rooms. The Germans checked each one. Now it was the turn of the French teacher. Glasseye peered at the curly-haired woman, "Are you Jewish?" he asked.

It was me they were after!

"*Mais non! Que pensez-vous!* I am Francaise!"

"You are from Lvov?"

"I am from Paris!"

I had to sit down, press my shaky knees together and clench my teeth.

Glasseye ordered Hans to search the room. "What's that?" Hans asked, opening an old cigar box containing the teacher's jewelry.

Glasseye looked. "Junk," he said. "Let's move on," and turning to the landlady he asked: "Who lives next door?"

"Mr. and Mrs. Bielinski."

"Not interested. We're looking for a single girl."

There were only two rooms left, none occupied by a single girl. It had narrowed down to me. They must have realized by now that I was the one. Why didn't they come out with it?

"You haven't checked me," I cried.

Both Glasseye and Hans stared at me. "You know the girl is right? Your papers, young lady!"

"My papers are in my room," I lied. "Two clients of Vinetta, the *German* firm I am employed by, are occupying it. *Herr* Berler asked me personally to see to it that those out-of-towners have a place for the night."

"Let's search her room anyway," Glasseye said.

They roused the two buyers. As soon as Widerko took out his identification papers and his work card, Glasseye grabbed his wallet and emptied the contents. A bundle of banknotes fell onto the table. Then Hans yelled at me, "Come on, come on, we haven't got all night!"

I produced my papers together with a voucher, signed and stamped by the Roman Catholic church and by the mayor of Bratkovka, asserting that "my ancestors" on both sides had been Roman Catholic for three generations. Hans handed the papers to Glasseye who gave them only a cursory glance. Then he looked at my wristwatch. "Don't you know Poles are not allowed to wear jewelry? I have to confiscate your watch."

"All my fellow-workers wear jewelry and our boss, a *German,* has never said a word to us."

"It's a new law," Glasseye said. "Your boss may not be aware of it yet.

I unclasped the watch and handed it to him The little diamonds sparkled in the light and Hans said, "They're real. Better give us whatever other jewelry you have. You'll save yourself a lot of trouble."

I would have given them the two bracelets and two gold chains in the drawer of my night table, but that would have made the Ukrainians and Poles suspicious because they never gave up their valuables without a fight. "I have no jewelry," I said.

"If we find anything you'll regret it," Glasseye said. Then he snapped at Hans: "Search! Take the closet and I'll take the chest."

Hans opened the closet and with two swift movements scooped out the heap of shoes and the electric cooker and let them fall cluttering to the floor. Hans squattted down, put his hand into a brown and then a white shoe. My heart in my mouth, I saw him reach for the electric cooker. Inside the screwed base, I had hidden thirty twenty-dollar gold coins.

"All worthless junk," Glasseye said. "Your pocketbook!" He grabbed it, turned it upside down and everything tumbled onto the table. He picked up the snapshot of Mark. "Come Hans, look at this Jew. This is a Jew. Who is he?"

"A friend, but he's not a Jew."

"And the child?"

"His."

"They're Jews and so are you."

"They're Poles and so am I."

"If you keep lying, we shall take you in."

I took a deep breath and said: "I wish you would. The police will clear this up."

"Aren't you afraid? You may never come back."

"Why? I haven't done anything wrong. Here, take my trinkets!" I said, and jerking open the night table drawer, I took from under scarves and handkerchiefs the two bracelets and the two chains and threw them on the table.

Glasseye scooped up my jewelry, Widerko's money and our documents and stuffed them into the pockets of his green-gray uniform. "Nobody is permitted to leave the house until morning! You'll get your papers back tomorrow, if, of course, we find everything is in order." They turned and left my room. I heard their steps down the stairs and then the slam of the outside door.

Widerko dropped his face into his hands. "The money is not mine. It belongs to the company," he cried.

I was unable to move. They said they'd be back tomorrow and maybe by then they would know I was not Cecylia Szarek. I ran to the bathroom, locked myself in, tore up the photographs of Mark and Bruno and threw the pieces into the toilet bowl. I reached for the porcelain handle dangling on the chain and pulled it.

The noise of the splashing water and the sight of the torn pieces being flushed down made me feel I was murdering my husband and my child.

Then the noise stopped and I saw a shred of paper still whirling in the foaming water. Half of Bruno's face was on it. I could almost hear his voice: 'Mummy, don't leave me.'

I reached in and plucked it from the water.

Just then somebody knocked and I shoved it into the neck of my dress. I shivered as the cold drops ran between my breasts. To camouflage the reason for which I happened to be in the bathroom, I pulled the handle again, slammed down the toilet seat and shouted: "I'll be out in a second."

Now, all the boarders were gathered in the living room discussing the event. One of them claimed that we had been victims of a plain ordinary holdup. He suggested to me that I call the police to find out. I refused. Then, without consulting the victims, he rang up the police and the Gestapo. He returned triumphantly to the living room. Neither authority had any knowledge of a search warrant for the boarders of Hoza Street.

And I had destroyed the photographs! The only ones I had.

I ran to the place of my crime, as if I could undo that which I had done. Anyway, it was the only place where I could let myself go. Clutching the piece of photograph I had rescued, I wept.

Back in the living room, I hoped that the tenants would account for the state I was in to the loss of my jewelry. They were all talking at the same time and had already decided what was to be done. The three victims, Widerko, his colleague and I, were to go the next morning to the police to report the robbery.

"They're Germans. We'll get back nothing! Why bother . . ." I protested.

"What can we lose?" Widerko said. "The police may catch the bandits. It's the only hope we have to get our money and your jewelry back. Don't you mind losing it?"

"Of course, I do." I wanted to say something stronger, but nothing came to my mind.

"So that's settled," Widerko said. "First thing in the morning we're going to the police, Miss Szarek. And now, let's get some sleep."

"All right." What else could I do? The net hau closed around me.

It was midnight before we went to bed.

Five times I dressed to flee, but where could I go? I had no place to hide.

I could not fall asleep for hours. When I finally did, I had a nightmare. An eye haunted me, it grew and grew, rolled like a stone towards me, to crush me.

6

O n the way to the Criminal Police Headquarters, I turned
from Widerko on my right to his companion on my left, flirting
with both so that they would not notice how scared I was.

On account of the bandits' German nationality, the Polish
police directed us to the German police.

Widerko knocked at the door of Room 313 on the third floor
and nudged me to enter first.

A German in uniform got up from behind his desk to shake
hands with us. "Rolf Rechter," he introduced himself.

He was thin, the upper part of his body somewhat bent
forward as if reaching out for something. When he focused his
penetrating eyes on me, I feared I would not be able to hide the
truth from them.

Widerko suggested I be their spokesman.

I had to swallow before I could bring out a word. "Well . . . I
am still upset from yesterday. Please, forgive me. Instead of being
asked questions I'd prefer to tell you what happened." Stuttering,
swallowing, pausing, I finished the story.

Rolf Rechter had me describe the bandits and said, "I promise
to do everything in my power to arrest those two crooks. What a
shame that German soldiers should commit such crimes! I hope I
will be able to return the stolen property to you."

Little did he know how much I hoped he would fail in his
search. If the crooks were arrested wouldn't they lead him to the
"single" Jewess from Lvov?

I reminded the German that the bandits had also taken our identification papers. Without them Widerko could not go home to Lvov. Without papers anybody was in trouble.

In the end Rolf Rechter supplied us with temporary certificates. What an unexpected stroke of luck! An identification paper endorsed with seals of the German Criminal Headquarters would mean a new lease on life for me. In a raid, or anywhere, no German, and certainly no Pole, would question the authority of the German police.

7

Papers were not enough to make me secure.

Anybody giving me more than a casual glance on the street made me catch my breath.

When Fischer appeared, I lost my self-control. "I can't bear it any longer," I said to him. "I am so scared. What if the bandits are caught? And that Rechter! You should have seen his eyes! It was as if he were looking straight through me. I'd better leave Warsaw."

"Where can you go?"

"Back to Lvov."

"You're out of your mind."

"Or to the Warsaw Ghetto."

"Good Lord!" Fischer exclaimed.

"I've heard that some people can adjust to living in the Ghetto."

"It's not a sanctuary, it's a hell."

"I'd share it with thousands of others of my own people. I wouldn't have to lie and pretend. I could weep openly. Here, Roma Brand is suffocating."

"Cecylia!"

"I must say it!"

"You must pull yourself together!"

"For what? It was for Bruno. Now, I don't even know where Bruno is. For myself alone I can't muster the strength to lie constantly and deceive people I've come to respect. I'm not a liar, and I'm not good at it. One day, a simple remark will trip me."

"You are doing fine."

"I'm not. Only the other day the subject of marriage came up among the girls at the office. I said that they're in too great a hurry to get under the canopy. The girls broke into laughter. Fortunately, Zosia quickly replaced canopy with altar. If any of the girls had been a little more attentive this error could have finished me."

"Cecylia . . ."

"Another time was when the Italian Contessa was laid out in the living room of the boardinghouse. I had learned the *Pater Noster* by heart. I know how to handle the rosary and know how to make the sign of the cross but, what was I supposed to do when passing a casket? Do you know, Fischer?"

"I don't . . . I am a Protestant. What did you do?"

"I made the sign of the cross and murmured, 'In the name of The Father The Son and The Holy Ghost,' and I wished I were dead."

"I know. I understand what you're going through. Believe me, I understand. But you must not give up."

"I don't know . . ."

"Remember, it is a matter of survival."

"And if I survive, what will be left of me? How will I find Bruno?"

"You'll be the same old Roma. You'll find your child, perhaps Mark, and you'll still have a whole life ahead of you. But you must fight!"

I glanced at him and wondered: Did the strength of Protestant Fischer depend upon the strength of "Catholic" Cecylia Szarek?

He smiled his tender smile and embraced me. "I need you," he said. "I can never thank you enough for accepting me as I am. I know I am an ugly man. Now, I have even made an appointment with a dentist."

8

"Try to concentrate, Miss Szarek, perhaps you can recognize the bandits," Rolf Rechter said, handing me a bundle of photographs in Room 313.

I looked at one photograph after the other, all the time aware of Rechter observing me. Suddenly Glasseye stared up at me. I tried to appear indifferent, but Rechter said: "Is this him?" and moved from behind his desk.

"I think so . . . Yes, it's he," I said.

"Thank you, Miss Szarek."

"May I go now?"

"No, not yet." He pressed a buzzer.

He will have me arrested. He knows by now that I am the Jewish girl from Lvov. I saw myself shuffling alongside the other Jews, driven on by armed guards, and I heard again the distant call, 'I have something to tell you . . . something to tell you . . .'

But it was Rechter who was saying, "Let me tell you, the one you've recognized has been arrested. He is the leader of a gang responsible for sixteen hold-ups and three murders. They've stolen furs, diamonds, cameras and other things which are valued at 100,000 zlotys. We have it all upstairs. I've buzzed for somebody to take you there. I hope you find your belongings, but first I want you to identify the crooks."

A handcuffed Glasseye was brought in. Then Rechter's interpreter, a Volksdeutscher named Mr. Schleger, took me to look for my belongings. They were not there and I hoped that would close the case for me.

My hope dissipated when Rolf Rechter summoned me a few days later and we drove to a jewelry store where I found my diamond watch. However, even then the case was not closed. Rechter told me that he had to take the watch to Headquarters and would be in touch with me.

Upon my return to the office, Berler asked why Danka had not reported to work. She had recently moved and had not left a forwarding address. In the past, she had gone on escapades that sometimes lasted two or three days. On such occasions I had tried to cover up for her, believing that perhaps she had ways of slipping through the gates into the Ghetto where she went to see her Jewish fiancé. Now I did not know what to say to Berler. "All I know, is that Danka did not feel well," I said.

Then I received a post-card from her. It bore the rubber stamp of the Paviak, the main prison of Warsaw. She asked me to send her a food parcel, and not to tell her sister.

Danka in prison? For what? What if she were promised freedom if she became an informant?

As if this were not enough, once back after an errand with Berler, I found Rechter in my cubicle. He was repeating Polish words Zosia was teaching him. Zosia left quickly. Rechter seemed embarrassed. "I brought your watch," he said.

". . . But I would have picked it up. Thank you."

"You know, you played an important part in breaking this case. Your description and then the identification of the bandits did it. Tonight I'm going to celebrate my promotion in a nightclub. I've invited my interpreter and his Polish fiancée. Would you do me the honor of joining us?"

Go to a nightclub with a German? I fumbled with the watch. He reached to help me put it on. "No, thank you, I'll manage." Without looking at him I added. "I haven't danced since the war started and I mean to keep it that way. I've made a vow."

"We don't have to go to a nightclub. We can go to a restaurant."

Did I dare to say no —?

"Please . . ." he said.

"I have a backlog of work."

"You work evenings?"

"If I have to."

"I'll talk to *Herr* Berler and see that you get an evening off."

In 1939 a German newspaper falsely accused Poland of

sending out troops to attack a radio station in Kleivitz, and shortly after, on September 1, the Germans declared war on Poland. In view of the crisis my father approved of my suggestion to invest all his cash money in stock and I volunteered to go to Lvov to buy yard goods for our store in Niemirov.

A few days after my return the Germans were in the town.

Finally Hitler and Stalin reached an agreement in which Poland was to be divided between Germany and Russia and the demarcation line would be the River San in Przemysl. Fortunately Niemirov fell into the territory belonging to the Soviets and those units of the German Army who had advanced beyond the agreed-upon demarcation line were compelled to retreat.

While the Germans had been in Niemirov, Father had moved away from his home where he had been exposed to abuse by them and the local hoodlums. He asked me to join him in a beggar's hut, claiming that with me around he felt more secure, that my knowledge of the German language was helpful when facing the occupying force. Mark was definitely against my going, but after Father had been beaten up, he gave in.

Bruno played just as happily in the beggar's hut as he had at home. Often he pretended he was a daddy to Lisa, my brother Abner's little daughter. He acted as if he were a dentist when I made out that I had a toothache, and he ran from the hut to the barn and back a hundred times. Sometimes he hid in the lean-to and acted deaf to our calls, just like Mark, Father and Abner did, when they were afraid of being caught by the enemy.

His playfulness became a source of irritation to Mark. "He can learn nothing but bad manners here. Can't you see what's becoming of our child? You asked me and I agreed to come over for one night. Five have passed. Enough is enough. We're going home," he said, while Bruno had once more hidden in the lean-to.

I went inside and found Bruno behind a barrel filled with pickles. His cheeks rosy from excitement, his flaxen hair disheveled, he laughed heartily convinced I would never have found him had he not voluntarily revealed his presence.

I could see no harm in these childish pranks nor could I detect any change for the worse in his behavior.

I embraced him, rubbed noses with him and sent him in to the hut to mollify his father.

I restrained myself during Mark's derisive and insulting remarks against one or another member of my family, and hoped that whatever they heard they would keep quiet too. Bruno en-

joyed having so many people around him. The inconveniences for us in the new quarters — lack of privacy or waiting for the outhouse to be vacant — were adventures to Bruno. All my family tried to please Mark so that he would allow me and Bruno to stay with them. That's why his wishes and comforts always came before their own.

Our non-Jewish friend Trusievicz informed my father that he had been sentenced to death by the Germans for having been a council to the local Jewish as well as to the Polish administration. While my father was disguised as a beggar, he was accompanied by the real beggar to the village of Radroz. There he went into hiding in the shack of one of his former Gentile employees.

The three weeks that it took for the German units to retreat to the River San were a complete nightmare to the inhabitants of Niemirov.

And now after all that my family and friends had been suffering at the hands of the Germans, I had to go out with one of them.

In my dread I had one consolation: I might be able to extract from Rechter the reason for Danka Bracka's arrest and perhaps this would do away with my fear that she would one day disclose my identity.

I was grateful for Rechter's consideration for two things: He wore civilian clothing and did not take me to a restaurant *Nur fur Deutsche* (For Germans only). He took me to one which catered to Poles and Germans.

Mr. Schleger, Rechter's interpreter, and his Polish fiancée had already arrived.

Ever since I had become Cecylia Szarek, I had dreaded meeting new people much as an actor dreads opening night. The only difference was that if I were to miss a cue or bungle my lines, I would never appear before an audience again.

Schleger's fiancée was wearing a kelly-green, fitted, silk dress with a low neckline. A snake with a ruby eye glittered on her chest. Although she struck me as a rather stupid girl, I was afraid of her because Poles were more apt to spot a Jew than Germans.

I sat on the edge of the chair, tying and untying the narrow scarf at my neck. I wanted to believe that Schleger's fiancée would have no reason to suspect me since I was Rechter's date. Schleger appeared to be a good-natured fellow. He had a generous laugh that dimpled his chin. But as I well knew, lambs turned into lions when they spotted a Jew.

Rechter's appraising glances made me squirm.

"We're not at the office," he said in a gentle tone of voice. We're here for a pleasant evening. Let's drink to Schleger's and Vanda's happiness." We all drank.

"Where did you go to school?" Vanda asked.

"In Silesia . . ." I said to justify my knowledge of the German language and hid behind the centerpiece of pink carnations.

"I went to school here in Warsaw," Vanda said and giggled as if it were the funniest thing in the world. She turned whispering to Schleger and my heart missed a beat. Then she laughed again and said that it was really too bad we hadn't gone to a nightclub because she loved to dance. I muttered an apology for having spoiled her fun. My glass was refilled.

Rolf Rechter took my hand. I was surprised by the softness of his touch. "You must have a lot of courage," he said.

I froze.

"Actually you're a shy girl," he said, "And yet you handled the whole affair of the robbery competently."

"Yes, I'm shy," I said and leaned back.

Vanda was laughing hysterically and I noticed that Rechter's eyes narrowed. Then he smiled and once more refilled my glass.

The good food, the soft music and the wine that I had never drunk in such quantity before finally relaxed me. This Rolf Rechter, in his ill-fitting suit, was a friendly man.

"What does your father do?" he asked.

"He was a highway builder."

"Engineer?"

"No, contractor," I took a deep breath. "And your father?" I asked.

Lowering his voice, he answered: "I never knew my father. I was born out of wedlock."

"Did you say that to shock me?"

"Are you shocked?"

"No."

He smiled. "My grandparents brought me up. They had a stenography service. But I'll tell you about myself some other time." He bent over his glass.

The gray-blue eyes that I remembered as hard and penetrating were now warm and caressing as he looked at me.

I tasted the *Sauerbraten* and dumplings I had ordered to please Vanda who had claimed it was her favorite dish.

Later when I accompanied her to the ladies room she suggested that I use make-up. "You look so drab," she said.

So much the better, I thought. My drabness would make her appear more glamorous and she would have no reason to dislike me.

When we returned to the table I felt almost peaceful. The music was sweet, the carnations glowed on the tables, the dimple-chinned Schleger and the solicitous Rechter seemed adorable. I found myself again in a world like the one I had known, it seemed, a long time ago — a world where I had been safe. The violins sang, *"Tausend kleine Võglein singen, habt euch lieb* (A thousand little birds are singing, you should love each other)." A table of young people roared: *Tief im Herzen hõr ich's klingen, habt euch lieb* (Deep in my heart I hear it ringing, you should love each other)."

Vanda and Schleger locked their arms and rocked to the music, Rechter tapped in rhythm and I sang out, *Habt euch lieb* (We should love one another)."

9

Although it was only one o'clock in the afternoon it had grown so dark in my cubicle that I had to switch on the electric light. I put the letters which I had been translating aside and took out my sandwich. The butter smelled rancid. I held my nostrils and bit into it.

If I weren't avoiding Rechter I could have fetched an *Eintopfgericht* (a bowl of soup with fresh vegetables and tiny chunks of meat) from the Gondola. However, since our evening together a few weeks ago the world had returned to "normal." I had decided to keep him at a distance.

The girls in the office, however, not only liked him but did not want to lose contact with such an influential person. Frequently they invited him for lunch at the Gondola and resented it each time I remained behind. Apparently, Rolf Rechter had made it clear that he accepted their invitations only in the hope of seeing me. They tried to make up for my absence by catering outrageously to his whims, by keeping him amused, raving when he played the piano in the restaurant.

They had already been rewarded for their efforts. For example, Rechter had intervened and freed Zosia's cousin who had been due to be sent to a Labor Camp in Germany.

Just as I finished my sandwich, Zosia burst into the office. "Guess who sends you regards?"

"I don't know."

"Rolf Rechter. He lunched at the Gondola as usual, but this

time he was *my* guest. He insisted that we bring you along tomorrow. I promised."

I turned to the window so that she would not see me blush.

"I don't understand how you can resist him," she went on. "He's terrific. I wish he'd fall for me. What have you got against him for God's sake?"

"I am a Pole. They have invaded our country. They have conquered us. Rechter is one of them. I can't forget. Can you?" I gave a prim little smile.

"Rolf is an exception, a decent guy. He proved that when he helped my cousin. I like him," Zosia said.

"He helped one," I said, "but how many did he harm?"

"That's too complicated for me," she answered. "If a good man, and a handsome one at that, asks me for a date I accept and I wish you would too. We don't get much of a chance to have fun."

"He's all yours," I said shortly.

"We've all tried to get him, don't worry. But no dice. He sits there all the time watching the entrance door. Anyway," she stopped to take a breath. "Why do you always eat lunch in the office?"

"I'm behind in work, Zosia," I said impatiently.

At that moment Berler stepped into my office and said, "Meet your old friend. Miss Maria Lasocka."

My heart jumped into my throat. Danka's replacement was no other than Mira Hendler, a Jewish cashier at the Lvov firm where we had both been employed during the Russian occupation.

"She said she knew you and we gave her a job," Berler said.

We shook hands woodenly. My boss asked me to show Maria around and left us. Zosia followed him.

"What is your name again?" I gasped.

"Maria Lasocka."

"I'm Cecylia Szarek."

"I know," she said. We stared at each other open-mouthed.

"When did you arrive? How did you get to Vinetta?" I asked.

She shrugged.

"Your husband and child are here too?"

"I came here with Brustiger, your old landlord. He calls himself Kovalski now."

"Did Brustiger, I mean Kovalski, tell you anything about my Bruno or Mark?"

"I never spoke with him about your relatives."

She had changed little. She still had that charming smile and her main interest was herself.

We heard the rest of the office workers returning from lunch and agreed to meet after work.

We met two blocks away from the Vinetta offices and went to see Brustiger-Kovalski.

A skinny and pale Kovalski embraced me. He had been caught in a raid in Lvov, and put into the Yanovska Death Camp from which Teichholz, a man of the Lvov *Judenrat,* had helped him — as many others before him — to escape. Kovalski shared the common belief that all of us would perish. Then he said: "I knew I could rely on you to get Maria the job."

I had never recommended Maria for a job in Vinetta. She must have heard of the firm from Kovalski. I noticed her double chin trembling and did not ask any questions. "Tell me, Kovalski, did you hear from my child, my husband?"

"Not a thing," he said. "Cecylia, stop crying."

"I might decide to move to the Ghetto," I sobbed.

"Do you know what's going on in the Ghettos?" Kovalski said. "The Lvov Ghetto has been burned to the ground."

"What —?" I shuddered. "But I can't bear it here any longer. I'm going to join the others behind the walls. I belong with them."

"Cecylia, there's worse to come," Kovalski said. He put his hands on my shoulders, fixed his eyes as if trying to hypnotize me, and added: "The Germans have decided to make Poland *Judenfrei* (clear of Jews)".

"What does that mean?"

"Death for all Jews."

"I don't believe it," I shouted. "They'd rather keep us working, squeeze every drop of blood out of us. Besides there are three million Jews in Poland. It's technically impossible to kill that many people."

Kovalski didn't answer.

"Remember Dreyfuss?" I cried.

"She doesn't understand," Maria said.

"You have a better chance than any of us," Kovalski said. "You look like a real Aryan."

"I feel I'd be better off with counterfeit papers like yours." I heard the frantic tone in my voice and tried to control myself.

"Don't give up, Cecylia," Kovalski said softly. He came and embraced me once more.

On my way home I decided that somehow or other I had to get the terrible news to the Ghetto and to my family in Niemirov and Rava-Ruska.

10

After tossing in bed for hours I realized that Blume, my youngest sister, was the only one I could save. My father, my step-mother, my sisters Anna and Adela, my brother Abner, his wife and their little daughter Lisa would be detected as Jews by their appearance alone.

I knew there were places in Warsaw where, for a certain fee, forged identification papers could be obtained. Kovalski introduced me to Julek, an "Aryan" like myself, who bought a birth certificate for Blume bearing the name of Frania Stanislavska, born in Warsaw. Julek also provided me with a Polish courier who was to deliver the documents to Blume in Niemirov and bring her to me.

The courier returned without her. She had refused to leave as yet. I could not blame her for she had no idea that time was running out. I had not been able to bring myself to mention the fate that lay in store for the Jews. Instead I sent a letter describing Warsaw as the most attractive city in the world.

Time passed mercilessly. I was mad with impatience for Fischer's next visit. He would be able to go to Blume and tell her the truth.

But when he finally did come, he refused.

He had been summoned by the Lvov Gestapo and they had grilled him. In the end he was cleared — but frightened.

"What did they accuse you of?" I asked.

"I told you, they cleared me . . ." he said.

"But what was it they cleared you of?"

"Don't be so inquisitive. Cecylia, I am here and alive —"

I was sure he had been accused of being Jewish. "Don't go back to Lvov, Fischer," I said. "Stay in Warsaw."

"Not only have I been cleared," Fischer said, "but the investigator praised me for the loyalty I've shown to my firm. He even congratulated the company for having me on the executive board." Two spots of color churned in his cheeks.

"Fischer, please remain here," I said.

"That would be running away, and I don't panic," he said. He grinned. "It's a good rule for you to remember."

Two weeks later Fischer was arrested.

"Since everybody knew of our friendship and that I had gotten my job through him, I waited for them to come for me too.

Suddenly I understood why he had never admitted to me that he was Jewish. If I didn't know — they could never squeeze it out of me and thus I would be safe.

So let them come. Let it be that way. If it hadn't been for Fischer I'd have remained in Lvov and would be deported now. He had attacked my complacency, had worn down my reluctance to become an imposter, had made me believe there could be a future. It was he who had stood by when "Cecilia Szarek" was making her first steps in a strange world, and it was he who had helped me to get the job in Warsaw. I felt as if it were part of a supreme justice that I should fall with him.

It would happen sooner or later anyway. I was convinced of it. The German Army had entered Lvov in June 1941 and now in August 1942 they were well on their way to Stalingrad. They were winning on all fronts.

How much longer would it take for me to make just one more wrong move? The pretense was driving me crazy. I wanted more than ever to go to the Ghetto. Whatever was to be the fate of the five-hundred-thousand inhabitants would also be my fate.

But who would Blume turn to when she arrived in Warsaw and I was gone?

I asked Berler what Fischer was accused of. When he implied that Fischer had embezzled large sums of money, I said firmly, "Impossible, not him!"

But a terrible suspicion arose in me. Recently Fischer had bought a lot of Vinetta merchandise and in order to get a discount he had paid for it in cash three months before the date of delivery.

Could it be that Berler wanted Fischer out of the way so that he could pocket a very considerable amount of money?

Berler was broke most of the time and nobody knew why. He'd gotten rid of his Polish partner with whom he had started the company, he now employed twenty-five people and was earning twice as much as before. What he did with his profits nobody knew. He frequently asked for and received loans from his employees. He gave parties in expensive restaurants but invitations were shunned because often a guest found himself paying out of his own pocket because Berler would claim that he was broke.

If he wanted Fischer out of the way, what would he do with me, who was the only witness to the cash deal? Perhaps he would not have me arrested now because Fischer's testimony and my testimony would bear each other out.

"Do you think the investigation of Fischer's case will get us involved?" I asked Berler.

"Possibly," he said. "It would be unpleasant for you because you two were great friends, I understand." He stared at the ceiling and played with the silver knob of his walking cane. Then he said, "There is a villa called June that has been put at my disposal as a vacation place for Vinetta employees. It is in Konstancin, just half an hour's ride on the local train. Why don't you go there for a little vacation until this unpleasantness blows over?"

I nodded and swallowed. I remembered that Berler lived in Konstancin which had formerly been a suburb for the wealthy, but where now all villas were closed, owners either having fled or preferred not to admit ownership. I was sure that I would be murdered at the desolated villa June.

"My caretaker will unlock villa June for you and see that you're comfortable. You'll be on leave starting tomorrow."

I had to go. There was nowhere I could hide.

That night, after I had packed a suitcase, I wrote to Blume telling her to get in touch with Maria upon her arrival in Warsaw.

The local train, leaving from Belveder Station, arrived in Konstancin thirty minutes later. Following Berler's directions, I walked up the empty Main Street, made two left turns and saw the woods ahead of me.

I went along a path in the woods. Sun filtered through the branches of the fir trees and birds were singing. I felt the peace, but also a terrible isolation.

I continued along the path until I finally came to a wrought-iron gate. At the far end of a driveway over which the tree branches arched, I could see patches of yellow wall. There was no sound except for the birds.

I turned the key in the lock of the gate and the noise startled me. I glanced behind. Nothing. The screeching of the rusty hinges seemed deafening.

My heart in my mouth, I approached the house.

Berler had given me three keys: One for the gate, one for the entrance door and a pass-key which would fit all nine rooms, three on the main floor and six upstairs.

I stepped into the hallway. The air smelled musty. I ran upstairs where I felt I would be safer. Anyone sneaking up to the house would not be able to look into my windows. When I reached the landing, I stopped and listened. Perhaps Berler was lying in wait for me? The deep silence made me shiver. I tiptoed to the nearest door, put my ear to it, looked through the keyhole and then opened it softly.

It was empty.

I chose a room that had a balcony overlooking the drive and the gate. Although the bed was made up, the room was almost bare. There were just a plain pine table and a wicker bench.

I threw open the glass door to the balcony to air the room and took a deep breath of pine-scented air. The branches of a tall pine tree leaned across the iron rail of the balcony and cones had dropped from them to the weather-bleached floor boards.

From up here, I could see a wild overgrown garden below. Even neglected as it was, it enchanted me despite my feeling of foreboding.

Later, I went to the general store I had noticed near the station to buy provisions.

Dusk caught up with me upon my return and for the first time in my life I found myself in the woods alone at dark. Frightened, I hurried along, ghosts at my heels. I reached the wrought-iron gate and, out of breath, fumbled with the lock, pushed it open and banged it shut. For a moment I felt safe. Approaching the house, however, I wondered whether the killer was waiting for me inside. I sneaked up the stairs, dashed into the room and turned the key.

On the glass panes of the balcony door the shadows of moving branches danced. The windows and the door to the balcony had no curtains. The next day I would buy packing paper to cover the windows so that I could turn on a light. I rummaged through my belongings for my flashlight, switched it on, took out the piece of

Villa Dziuna in the woods at Konstancin, near Warsaw where the author was hidden

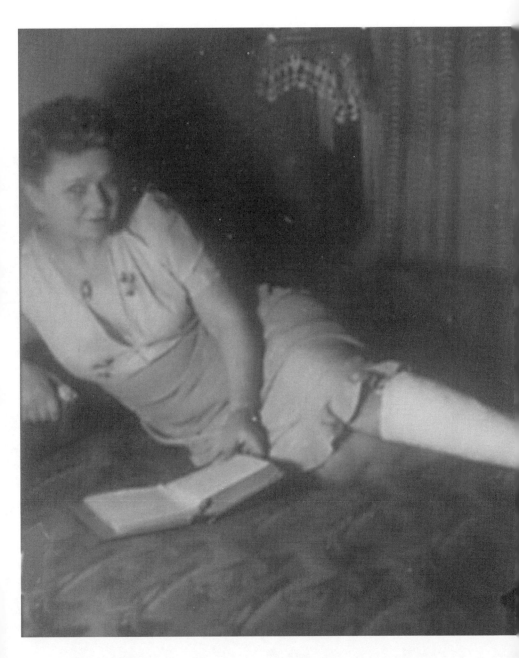

The author under the guise of "Cecylia Szarek" with broken leg

The first toy in my life — a gift from Rolf Peschel (1943)

*The author as "Cecylia Szarek" on the left with her sister Blume
Brand also living on false papers as the Catholic "Gloria
Wasilewska" (1942)*

Bruno's photograph, wiped some tears away and murmured: "At least my baby may be safe wherever he is."

I switched off the flashlight and placed it under the pillow. In the dark I ate a piece of bread and sausage and then I went to bed.

Sleep would not come.

I thought of Blume, a stranger in Warsaw, the first time away from her parents, all alone. Fischer had been at my side but who would be with Blume? Perhaps it had been wrong for me to insist that she come to Warsaw. I couldn't guarantee her safety. The precariousness of my situation could only be a threat to *her*.

Every little sound made me leap up — a gust of wind, the rustle of dry leaves. When a pine cone fell to the balcony floor I was out of bed pressing myself against the cold panes of the door. I even mistook my own breathing for an alien sound.

During the days I managed to control my nervousness but each night I imagined I heard a stranger tiptoe up the stairs.

Everyone at Vinetta knew where I was and I waited anxiously for word from Maria that Blume had arrived.

On Sunday the sound of girlish laughter made me dash to the window and look. Maria, Zosia, and Vaclava Ksiazkievicz, the bookkeeper, were standing behind the gate. I called out to them excitedly and hurried downstairs and down the drive to open the gate for them.

All three simultanously started to tell me the latest news from Vinetta. I found a moment alone with Maria and asked if she had heard from Blume. But there had been no news from her and no news regarding Fischer's case. Rolf Rechter, however, had dropped into the office and had been surprised not to find me.

"We didn't tell him where you were," Zosia said. "That's what you wanted, right?"

Maria added: "Berler might have told him when he had dinner with him at the Gondola."

They had brought frankfurters and *sauerkraut* which we heated on an electric hotplate. The girls were disappointed that their vacation place had not yet been supplied with dishes and they said they had imagined it to be much more luxurious but they didn't seem to mind eating off a table covered with brown packing paper, drinking tea out of flower vases and saucepans, and using their fingers instead of knives and forks. They frolicked on the lawn and the driveway and Zosia even crawled into the dog-house and stuck her tongue out at us. Exhausted, they left at nightfall, promising to come again the following Sunday.

Alone, in my room, I stared at the shadows on the window-shades. It seemed to me that I saw Fischer's profile with its broken nose. Had he managed to keep his appointment with the dentist before he was arrested? I would always see him in my mind's eye with a front tooth missing.

11

"**H**urry, please hurry!" I called to the man who was driving me in a vehicle that looked like a rickshaw.

Blume had arrived and gone to a hotel, thus making herself the target of the police-inspection. She tried to reach me at Vinetta and, luckily, it had been Maria who answered the telephone.

I burst into her room.

We hugged one another, laughing and crying at the same time.

She started to tell me the news but I interrupted her. "We have to leave this place at once. Just tell me whether you've heard from Mark."

"No. But Father and Perele . . ."

"Not now. Take your things and let's get out of here. For God's sake, why did you check into a hotel?"

Blume's eyes grew wide. "But Jan Kulok who brought me here suggested I stay at a hotel until I was able to get in touch with you."

"Who's Jan Kulok? Does he know who you are?"

"Of course not. Anna told him that I was her friend's daughter, not her sister, and asked him to keep an eye on me during the trip because I was only eighteen years old. He's a very nice man."

"As long as he doesn't know, it's all right."

I rushed her down the stairs, but when we neared the lobby, I told her to walk slowly. Outside I hailed a rickshaw.

"Belveder Station," I ordered.

"You know what?" Blume whispered, "Last night at the hotel they banged on my door. Two Polish policemen walked in and asked for my papers. So I showed them that birth certificate you sent me and, of course, I told them that I had a matching baptismal certificate . . ."

"You what —?"

"What's wrong with that? I did have a matching —"

"Oh Blume!" I burst in. "Who will take care of you if something happens to me?"

"They called me *Lipa*," Blume said in a small voice. "What's that?" She looked frightened.

"It means phony," I said.

"Oh — Roma."

"Cecylia! Cecylia! Don't ever call me Roma again!"

Now her eyes filled with tears.

"You must forget our old names. You must forget we are sisters. You must forget our past." I looked at her sternly. "You are Frania now — even in your sleep."

Frania cried.

I realized what a child she was and how very old I had grown. I put my arm around her and I dried her eyes with my handkerchief. "It's difficult, my little darling, I know it's difficult for you . . ."

At the station I briefed her, "On the train we will not sit together. I will get off at a station called Konstancin and you'll follow me. We'll go to the house of my friend, Julek. You'll stay with him and his wife until I find a furnished room for you where you can live properly registered with the local police.

In a trembling voice Frania said: "If I had known we would not be together, I wouldn't have come."

I looked at her struck dumb at her pitiful ignorance and patted her shoulder. "I wish nothing more than that we could be together. But now it's impossible dear."

We boarded the train. Frania took a seat across the aisle from me and kept looking fixedly out of the window.

When the train pulled into the station of Konstancin, I let her off first then went slowly down the platform to give the other travelers time to disperse before joining her. I found her sitting forlornly on her suitcase just outside the station door. "You did very well, Frania," I said.

She didn't look up.

I picked up her heavy valise and carried it all the way to Julek's apartment.

When I visited her next she looked very pale. She had been confined to her room because Julek could not allow an unregistered guest to be seen in his apartment. She complained that she was only allowed to go to the bathroom they all shared late at night, when the whole building was asleep and no one could see her. I was tempted to tell her about Fischer's arrest, the reason I had been forced to go into hiding, and that a week ago Glassner and his accomplice had been transferred from the police to the military to be court-martialed and that I had been summoned as a witness. But why frighten the poor child more than necessary?

The next time I went to see Frania, Julek asked me to take her out of his apartment because, according to him, she looked semitic and, therefore, endangered his family's safety.

I had no other choice but to take her to villa June.

How would I cope with Berler's caretaker's sudden appearance at the villa, or what would I do in case Berler got wind of an uninvited tenant who had no connection with Vinetta? I put these questions out of my mind.

The first time I had seen the caretaker approach villa June, I had hidden under the bed because I took this strange-looking man for a hired killer. Later when I heard him hammering downstairs I realized it must be Schone, whom Berler had mentioned, and that he had probably come to do repairs. I went downstairs to introduce myself.

Schone was in his late thirties, wearing a gray suit, a gray wide-rimmed fedora, and tennis shoes. He stopped hammering and put a white handkerchief quickly to his nose. "Sorry, I have hay fever," he said. And, as if to prove it, he cleared his throat, blew his nose and coughed, keeping his face half-hidden in the handkerchief. He asked: "How long are you going to stay here?"

"Two weeks."

"What a place for a vacation . . ."

"I like the simple life."

"Aren't you cold? I'll bring an electric heater from Berler's villa. What else do you need?"

"I'll manage with what I've found here."

He gave me a suspicious look and I did not know what to make of it.

A few days later when he brought me the heater, I mentioned that I had invited a girl friend to spend a few days with me. "Perhaps I shouldn't have. Perhaps Mr. Berler wouldn't approve, but it's sort of lonely here," I said. "What do you say, Mr. Schone? I can still tell her not to come."

"I won't tell *Herr* Berler," Schone said, and shrugged.

Schone came every day under different pretexts to villa June. The day I brought Frania there, he was checking the roof for leaks.

His eyes examined Frania carefully and with a certain emphasis he asked: "Is *she* the friend you mentioned?"

"Yes —"

He smiled and, to my surprise, for the first time took his handkerchief from his face and stuffed it in his pocket.

I saw that he had an enormous hooked nose.

He settled himself on the wicker bench and, taking out his pipe, he asked Frania, "Where do you live?"

His manner indicated that he knew Frania was Jewish. I realized instantly that he must now suspect *my* real identity. The thing I had wanted to prevent was happening. To avoid further inquiries, I put a question to him: "Have you been working for Berler a long time?"

"Well," he said, "Some time ago I started working at Vinetta. Then Berler made me caretaker of his living quarters, villa Vera in Konstancin. I prefer the country, anyway." He cleared his throat and looked fully at me, "I am Jewish," he said.

Shocked that he had the guts to disclose his secret, we fell silent.

Then he went on to tell us that at one time he had been a lawyer in Cracow, that he was married, and that he and his wife lived separately because it gave her a better chance to survive. He pointed to his nose.

"It must surprise you that I would confide in you," he said. "But my secret eats away at me." He glanced at Frania and added: "Something makes me trust you."

What I feared, had happened. Schone knew.

"Does Berler know your secret?" I asked.

Schone shrugged. Obviously he did not want to disclose the kind of relationship he had with Berler. He turned his head to the side showing us his profile, and asked, "Don't you think my nose looks Roman rather than semitic?'

"It does," I agreed. "In Spain or France it might go unnoticed, but you know . . . Under the circumstances . . ."

I felt I ought to tell my own secret to him, but the usual fear would not let me do so.

After Schone left, Frania said, "Cecylia, I must tell you —"

"Let's unpack now," I said. I saw tears in her eyes.

"I must tell you about Niemirov," Frania said.

I didn't want her to go on. I was frightened of what she might tell me. But I sat down on the bed, and said, "Tell me . . ."

Frania wiped her eyes. "It was about two months ago," she began. "It happened in the morning. They came with four lorries and two cars and they stopped at the Market Place. From the window we saw eight Germans in uniform going to the *Judenrat*. Fifteen minutes later the Jewish Militia pasted up flyers everywhere, a decree stating that one hundred Jews over twenty-one must assemble at the Market Place within four hours. We kept watching. About thirty Jews came. Later there began a house to house search for seventy more Jews.

"Father decided to hide in the cellar and some neighbors, believing he deserved a special lease on the favors of Providence, also came along.

"My friend Golda Bruh and I pushed the dining table over the trap door to the cellar and we covered it with a large table cloth that hung almost to the floor.

"Afterwards Golda and I ran up to the attic and hid behind an old trunk. Suddenly we heard voices downstairs and we knew they were searching. Then we heard their steps near the attic stairs. I was sorry I hadn't gone to Warsaw. I couldn't understand how I could have been so foolish. I knew that if somehow I managed to get out of this situation, I would leave immediately."

"Go on, go on," I said.

"In the opening of the stairs the cap of a German appeared. Then his face then all of him. He had a gun in his hand. 'Anybody here?' he shouted.

"It sounded awfully loud. With his gun pointing, he looked this way and that. I called to him in German, and came out from behind the trunk and threw myself at his feet."

"You did what?" I asked.

"He would have found us anyway . . . He stared for a long time at me and asked how old I was. I told him and he said something about his sister.

"He waved his gun toward Golda who was watching us now

and hissed, 'Get back there.' Then he turned and went downstairs and I heard him say, 'Nothing up there!'

"We heard them tramp around and then there was silence. We stayed in the attic until we heard the lorries leave.

"When we returned downstairs, the dining table had been pulled away from the trap-door. We called down into the cellar, but nobody answered. We went down to look but nobody was there.

"Outside some Jews had gathered at the corner of Lubaczov Street. I didn't see Father among them. But I saw Abner running past. He looked at me for a moment wih a crazy expression. I asked. 'Where is Father?' His lips moved but he did not say a word and he ran on.

"Manek from the Jewish militia had been with the Germans searching our house. He had been under the mistaken impression that we had all run to the woods and that there was nobody home. At least that's what he claimed. To pacify the Germans who raised hell at that point because they hadn't found anybody, Manek pointed out the cellar trap-door. He said he could have killed himself when he saw Father. Lejzor Brand of all people!

"After Father, Perele, and our neighbors were taken to the Market Place, Manek looked for Abner and told him they would allow Abner as a member of the *Judenrat* to free one relative picked up in the raid."

In a voice that seemed not to be my own I asked. "Abner a member of the *Judenrat* —?"

"Father had refused the transfer from the city council to the *Judenrat*. So they insisted that Abner serve instead." She paused. "Well, where was I? Oh—

"Abner rushed to the Market Place and saw Father standing, rocking back and forth and chanting psalms. Abner started to pull Father toward the guards. But Father pushed him away and pointed at Sara who was sitting nearby on a sack. Abner hadn't known that his wife had also been taken. Father told him to get a release for Sara first. But Abner didn't move.

"Father had to shake him and tell him, 'Your first obligation is to your wife! Go, go, my son.' And then in a small voice, 'Afterwards, perhaps you can do something for me and my Perele . . .'

"Sara told me later that when Abner turned to her, Father began to chant again and rock back and forth, back and forth . . ."

I had Frania in my arms.

"Did Father ever write?" I asked.

"No."

"Does anybody know where they were taken?"

"To a labor camp, they say. The young people dig ditches and the old pluck feathers for quilts all day long."

"That's not so bad," I sighed.

"After a few days," Frania went on, "the three hundred of us who were left in Niemirov were ordered to move to Rava-Ruska. Luckily, we had Anna and Hersh there and they took us in."

Frania lay back on the bed.

"Hersh insisted that I go to you but Abner was against it. He said that my place was with them. 'You are as selfish as Roma,' he told me, and that made me feel awful. But Hersh signaled to me not to argue. Later Hersh told me that Abner was upset and didn't know what he was saying." She took a breath. "He isn't himself anymore, Roma. He even quarrels with Sara and yells at little Lisa . . . But before I left he was just sitting and brooding all the time."

"Did the Germans leave you alone in Rava-Ruska?"

"There was one *Action* after another. It was horrible. But Hersh had built a hiding place. he built a false ceiling where there was a crawl space for his mother, Anna, Adela, Sara and the baby and me to hide.

"Hersh and Abner were safe for the time because they had been designated as grave diggers. I can't tell you how awful it was to be crowded into the airless space with the Germans tramping inches above our heads. After my first experience of that I told Anna I wanted to go to you and Anna arranged for Jan Kulok to take me."

The shrill ring of the bell at the gate made us jump to our feet. There in the bright sun were Vaclava, Zosia, Maria and Kovalski.

"To the attic, Frania! This way." We ran out of the room, to the attic ladder in the corridor.

I watched her disappear, quickly powdered my tear-reddened face and went downstairs.

My friends saw that I had been crying. I told them that I had a terrible toothache and could do nothing about it since it was Sunday.

Zosia dug into her bag and produced two aspirins. "This will help," she said, as we came to my room. Then she motioned the girls out again and turned to Kovalski: "Let's go to the garden," she said. Kovalski didn't move. "Give her a slog of vodka," she said. "That will put her on her feet." And she left giggling.

Alone with Kovalski, I told him I had just received the news of my parents' deportation. He knew my father. He would sense what I was going through.

He put his arms around me. "Maybe they'll find Bruno," he said.

"Not Bruno!" I tore myself from his embrace. "Bruno is safe! Bruno is with a Catholic family somewhere near Zloczov."

I was sobbing.

"Cecylia, stop it. Do you want Vaclava and Zosia to suspect you? Powder your nose and let's join the girls in the garden."

12

The following Sunday Zosia came to villa June alone to warn me that, if I wanted to keep my job, I had better come back to work because Maria was trying to take over my place. She was spending more time in Berler's office than seemed justified, and lately she had been using my desk in the cubicle instead of hers which was in the filing department.

"Has there been any investigation in connection with Fischer's case?" I asked Zosia.

"Not that I know of."

"Nobody came to inquire about me?"

"You mean Rechter? Oh yes. He asked abouc you several times at the Gondola restaurant."

Monday I was back at Vinetta. As far as I could tell, Berler was glad to have me back. Perhaps he had given up the idea of getting rid of me? Perhaps Rechter's interest in me had stopped Berler from doing anything.

Although commuting every day was difficult for me, I had to live in villa June for Frania's sake. At the same time I found a new room in Warsaw in Vaclava's apartment. As long as Frania was not registered with the police she could not apply for a *Kennkarte* (identification card) and did not dare to walk the streets. Each morning I locked her in, leaving a spare key with her in case of an emergency. She was not to leave our room since, despite the isolation of the villa, somebody might come by and see her.

As a matter of fact workmen did come. They went about repairing the roof and the plumbing, and replacing broken windows. One day the plumber showed up late in the afternoon and hammered for an hour. The next day nobody came. The day after that the roofers clattered over our heads awakening us early in the morning. All Schone could do was to see to it that *our* room was not scheduled for any restoration work.

Frania had to be careful, not to sneeze or cough. She had to move about on bare feet so as not to arouse anyone's curiosity.

During the day at work my fear spun the most gruesome horror stories. My fantasies were so compelling that during the train ride home I always invented elaborate plans as to how to rescue her as if her arrest were inevitable.

Again and again I found Frania safe and one day I noticed that her face and arms were flushed with the sun. I knew that the pine trees kept the balcony shaded at all times. It was clear that she was not following my instructions that she should stay inside, but my sympathy for her confinement would not let me call her to task.

She had arrived with a small bulky cotton bag which she kept on a string around her neck inside her brassiere. At night she stuck it under the mattress. I knew she was trying to hide it from me. Perhaps Anna had given her a nest egg.

One night I kept tossing in bed, my body burning with an unnatural heat. The sheets seemed suffocatingly heavy. I threw them off. Even the gold chain holding a plain gold cross about my throat seemed an insupportable burden. Suddenly it was the drawstring of Frania's little cotton bag choking me. There was a hand pulling it tighter and tighter, Frania's hand growing grotesquely huge.

I screamed, and woke up shaking.

It took a long time, sitting up in bed, staring into the dark, before I was able to relax and go back to sleep.

What had made me see Frania as threatening?

Whenever I returned from work I would rush upstairs to find her, a little forlorn heap, on the bed and I would pull aside the blanket and the sheet and take her in my arms and comfort her. She would hug me and ask me how the day went without ever complaining about the terrible hours she had spent alone.

13

Through some mysterious influence Weinstein, the manager of Mrs. Lesnievska's antique shop downstairs, who was also connected with the Ghetto manufacturing firm of BBH, had a permanent pass to the Aryan part of the city and he was allowed to remain in charge of the antique shop in our building. We had met a few times but I tried to keep my distance.

When he entered my office, the armband on his sleeve was covered by a trenchcoat hung over his shoulders.

"Miss Szarek," he said softly, "I've come to ask you a favor."

"Yes?"

"Twenty-five of the BBH workers have been picked up and are being held at the *Umschlagplatz* (assembly point for the deportation of Jews from the Ghetto). God only knows where they'll be sent. Berler told me you have a German friend. Could he intervene?"

Why had he come to me? Did he guess I was Jewish? But if Weinstein had really suspected me, he would have told Mr. Korman of his discovery, and only two days before, on an inspection visit to the BBH warehouse in the ghetto, I had overheard Mr. Korman say to his partner in Yiddish, 'If not for this *goldene Shikse* (golden gentile woman), what would we do?"

"I am not in the habit of fraternizing with Germans," I said sharply.

(It must be explained here that for a Pole to become intimate with a German was regarded as a disgrace, and how much more was it for a Jew to do so! What if Weinstein suspected that I, a fellow-Jewess, had befriended a Nazi? It would be a total betrayal of our people.)

"Why should Rechter help?" I asked Weinstein.

"Miss Szarek, not one, not two, but twenty-five human beings are in danger. However slightly you know the men, you should use every influence to help."

My whole heart went out to Weinstein, to those twenty-five on the *Umschlagplatz*.

"*Herr* Berler told me that Rechter helped Zosia's cousin," Weinstein went on. "He seems to be a decent man . . ."

"There are no decent Germans," I snapped.

"All you have to do is ask him. Yes? We ought to help one another."

Why did he say *we*?

"Zosia's cousin is a Pole, *your* men are Jewish," I said, making my identification clear in case he may have suspected me.

"I beg you, Miss Szarek, talk to Mr. Rechter."

I shrugged, pretending to give in in order to get rid of Weinstein.

Rechter answered the phone. I asked if I could speak to him immediately.

"Of course!" he sounded radiant. "Just give me a minute to change into civilian clothes."

"This time I'd like to see you in uniform because it's about official business. I'll be in your office within twenty minutes."

Weinstein had already picked up my raincoat and was holding it out to me. "Take an umbrella," he said considerately, "it's coming down heavily. And Miss Szarek," he added in a strange tone, "no sacrifice on your part is too big if it buys the lives of twenty-five innocent people. God bless you."

In Rechter's office I talked quickly. "Too many workers of BBH have been deported. We can't keep up with our orders. Our customers are complaining. If we lose more workers we'll suffer a big financial loss, not to speak of the trouble it will bring us. Mr. Berler asked me to see you," I lied. "He was wondering whether you could do anything to get those twenty-five Jews back to work."

I saw Rechter frowning and I added quickly: "They may be only Jews, but they're skilled and absolutely irreplaceable."

"The Fourth Department of the Gestapo is the special division that handles Jewish affairs," Rechter said. "The chief of the section is *Sturmbandfuhrer* Brand. It is possible that one of my colleagues may know him personally. Excuse me for a moment."

The same name as mine! It was macabre to say the very least.

Rechter returned and asked me to follow him. Outside, he hailed a rickshaw. "To the Ghetto,' he said.

"Which entrance?" the driver asked.

"I'll direct you."

The driver pedaled hard. The rain drummed on the canvas roof. Rechter looked grim.

"Will you be able to do something?" I asked.

"My colleagues advised me not to, but I've already called *Sturmbandfuhrer* Brand and he has agreed to let the twenty-five workers go. You'll have to identify them."

"I? I don't know them," I said and gasped at my admission.

"There's no time to call someone who does," Rechter said. "We'll have to try to trace them."

The rickshaw bumped and I was thrown against him. His hands steadying me confused me. Rechter asked: "Do you have a Ghetto pass?"

"Oh God, I don't have it with me. I didn't know . . ."

"We'll go directly to the *Umschlagplatz*. I can get you in there."

When Rechter stopped the driver, I opened my umbrella and stepped out into the mud.

"Watch your step," Rechter said and took me by my arm. "It's slippery." He guided me around the deeper puddles toward what was called no-man's land, an uninhabited section of the Ghetto.

There in the gray mist Germans in uniforms appeared dimly and behind them there was a long dark line that seemed to be part of the landscape, but it was moving. It was a column of ragged human forms weighed down by bundles, shuffling along. A small child clung to the hand of a thin, bent figure.

"Wait here, I'll be back in a minute. I am just going to get the 'go-ahead' from *Sturmbandfuhrer* Brand," Rechter said.

Rechter was gone and I, holding my umbrella, stood alone in the rain.

A creature stepped out of the column and threw itself in the mud before the group of uniformed men. I heard a whimpering. The men ordered it to get up. Then a shot rang out and the whimpering stopped.

Perhaps I cried out, for two of the men turned and headed toward me.

"*Passierschein* (Pass to the Ghetto)!" one of them said.

My knees were trembling "I don't have my pass with me." I said. "I am an employee of Vinetta. I am here on behalf of *Herr* Berler. I came with an investigator of the *German* Police." The words rolled out as if from a machine.

"Where is he? You are a Jewess, aren't you?"

I tried to keep my voice steady. "Would I have come here if I was a Jew? I am Polish!"

"*Kennkarte* (identification paper), please."

I reached into my purse, got out the temporary identification paper and my working card and handed them both to the interrogator.

They peered at me and at the photograph of my work card. And then the interrogator said, "Follow us."

"Mr. Rechter will be back any minute," I pleaded.

What made him grin like that?

"Get moving!" he said. Sandwiched between the two, I was led toward a four-story building where about twenty Jews, their arms raised above their heads, were lined up facing the gray brick wall.

Other rain-drenched Jews sat on a long log. Some had their faces buried in their hands, others stared unseeingly.

A shocked witness only a few minutes ago, I was one of them now, the stray sheep restored to the fold.

What would become of Frania?

"Please, wait just one more minute," I pleaded to the two Gestapo men. "Or take me to *Sturmbandfurer* Brand."

The name Brand seemed to electrify them. They whispered together and then the interrogator took off. The other ushered me into the drab entrance-way of the administration building. I made a supreme effort to appear annoyed, as a Pole would. I went straight to one of the wooden benches and, counting the fateful minutes, stared at the brown doors, the mud-smudged linoleum floor and the stone steps leading upstairs.

In 1941, when the Germans came to Lvov and ordered all Jews to wear the white armband bearing the blue Star of David, I was attacked on the street by a few Poles who accused me of being a Catholic sympathizer of the Jews, and it took some maneuvering to get away from the threatening mob.

All this happened because of my so-called "good looks," an

expression which at that time meant an appearance that was not specifically Jewish and had nothing to do with physical attractiveness. Because of my non-Jewish features, my friend congratulated me on my excellent prospects of survival.

And now, without the armband and with Catholic papers, I was arrested as a Jew.

What if Rechter had a hand in this? I realized all at once how much I liked Rechter, and that such a betrayal would be unbearable to me.

When I heard his voice outside and saw him step through the door, I had to keep myself from rushing into his outstretched arms.

He was pale. "Cecylia! I had to wait for *Sturmbandfuhrer* Brand. That's why it took me so long." He took me by my hand and turned to the interrogator: "We will go to find the Jews," he said, and to me, "Let's go, Miss Szarek."

On the way to the exit, he lowered his voice: "How dreadful! What a frightening experience! If something had happened to you, I would never forgive myself." The pressure of his fingers on mine was fierce. "Thank God I came in time. Thank God," he repeated. "And look," he showed me a paper, "I have Brand's permission to take twenty-five BBH workers out of here."

It had stopped raining. Masses of gray clouds were racing overhead. Rechter stepped over to the Jews sitting on the log. "Any workers of the BBH among you, stand up!"

None moved.

How could I signal to them that this was no trap? Their fearful eyes told me what they were thinking. Only one pair of black eyes belonging to a young lad looked up boldly. To Rechter I said, "Perhaps they don't understand German, may I say it in Polish?"

Rechter nodded.

"We have permission to *free* twenty-five BBH workers. Step forward!"

Four of those standing against the wall dropped their raised arms and turned.

"Step over here," Rechter called.

They staggered to his side clutching their arms.

"Who else?" I asked, peering into each face separately. "BBH workers step forward," I repeated.

Two more men turned from the wall, but none of those sitting on the log reacted. More and more frantically I ran back and forth, from the men on the log to those along the wall. "There must be twenty-five BBH workers among you," and I quickly added in

Polish: "We have permission to *free* twenty-five — forget about BBH — grab this chance!"

I burned to say a few words in Yiddish but did not dare in front of Rechter. I searched for one single word, a clue for these people that a friend spoke. Silently I pleaded with my father to hand me one word.

I hurried over to the black-eyed lad and riveting my eyes to his, I uttered: *"A'vade,"* the Yiddish word for 'of course'. To cover myself in front of Rechter, I added in German, *"Ihre Wade ist sichtbar* (Your splintbone is visible)."

The youth was on his feet. He whispered something to the others. Then he marched forward and joined the group of six at Rechter's side.

One by one others came forward. But only twenty-one dared to take advantage of this chance.

Rechter lined them up and guided them out of the *Umschlagplatz* in the direction of the inhabited Ghetto. Then he handed the man in the lead the document signed by Brand. "Take these people to the BBH and report back to work."

As they left, the young fellow smiled at me and removed his cap with an ever so slight bow, as though he wished to thank me.

Rechter and I watched them until they were out of sight.

"Thank you, *Herr* Rechter," I said.

"Let Berler thank me for his workers. It's all part of official business isn't it?"

"Please . . . It's not necessary to be so formal. *I* am thanking you for him."

"Your thanks are certainly more welcome than Berler's could ever be," he said warmly. And, taking my hand, he led me out of the Ghetto.

Weinstein asked twice more to have Rolf intervene on behalf of BBH workers. Twice more Rolf succeeded. Once fourteen "indispensible" workers were released from the *Umschlagplatz* and then twelve were released. But I did not go back to the Ghetto with him.

14

"Try to speak a little softer, Frania, and without gesticulation," I said.

It was Sunday, and I was watching the gate through the window of villa June. For Frania's sake we had to keep vigil as one of my co-workers could appear to spend the day in the country at any time.

"You think you know everything," Frania said. "My Polish teacher in Niemirov talked with her hands more than any Jew I know."

In normal times one could make allowances for teenage rebellion, but in our situation our very lives were at risk. Polish squads had been trained to weed out imposters in the streets, the tramways, and the restaurants, and they were being paid for each catch they brought to the Gestapo.

No matter how obnoxious my insistence seemed to Frania, I could not allow myself the comfort of being lax. Some day she would make her own choices, her own decisions, and her own mistakes, but now she had to stay alive, even if she ended up hating me.

"You see this muff, Frania?" I said. "Because I talk with my hands, too, I keep my hands locked together inside it. I only regret that muffs are not worn in the summertime or in offices."

Poor Frania! But, much as I felt for her, she made me impatient, swallowing all of Schone's flattery about her "Gentile good looks" rather than listening to my warnings that she should not show her face unless it was absolutely necessary.

The important thing was that her resentment should not become her own undoing.

I went to her, put my arm around her in a half embrace, and went with her back to the window where we stood looking out for a time in silence. I suddenly thought of Father. If he could have had one wish he would have wanted Blume (now Frania) to survive. He believed that she would follow his bent toward orthodoxy. Then, all at once, I thought — the *Kennkarte* (identification paper)!

In order to get such a document one had to present oneself for examination. Frania had come only recently to Warsaw and would be sure to come under suspicion. Before undergoing such a check-up, even Poles were extremely nervous, whilst imposters underwent traumas. Frania, to whom I had spoken about it, showed no trepidation.

Julek, Kovalski, Maria and I had endlessly discussed the whole situation — what to say, how to say it, what not to say, and how to fill out the application forms. I had been advised that the best approach was to behave casually but not to overdo it.

Some, like Schone, realizing that just how semitic they looked, could not bring themselves to submit their application in person. They bought a counterfeit *Kennkarte* on the blackmarket.

"Frania, we have to rehearse the answers to the drilling," I now said.

"I know what to say," she answered, drawing away from me. "I'll know what to do when the time comes."

I said nothing, just went to our only bed, stretched out and closed my eyes. I let my thoughts drift, to another time, to another place.

"Please Mark, bear with it a little longer," I pleaded. "I will make it up to you somehow, please?"

"Why, you're more concerned with your family's well-being than with your son's!"

"Bruno will be all right. Anyway, I promise, I will double my efforts after the war is over."

"I'll never stay with your relatives in a beggar's hut that long."

"I didn't mean it that way. I simply wanted to tell you that then I'll devote myself entirely to you and Bruno, and make up for the time we've lost. All right, Mark? But now my relatives are desperately in need of help."

"Why are they so important to you?"

"Isn't your family to you? Come on now, let's have lunch. We have corn-on-the-cob today and you and Bruno like it so much."

Shouts to open up and harsh pounding on the door prevented Mark from answering me. He disappeared immediately in the lean-to, and I called Abner from the other room to follow him. Then I opened the door.

Two Germans in uniform and one Ukrainian had come for Father.

"Mr. Brand is not here," I said.

They ransacked the attic, the cellar and the lean-to. They made Mark and Abner come out. One German, addressed by the other as Kurt, asked them how they were related to Lejzor Brand, and upon learning that one was the son and the other the son-in-law, they ordered them to come along.

Mark, slow in complying with the order, was shouted at: "Are you hard of hearing? Judenschwein *(Jewish swine)! Otto kick him out."*

Mark quickly moved on and I followed close behind them, wondering whether Mark and Abner were being taken instead of Father.

Kurt whispered something into the Ukrainian's ear. The latter departed and disappeared into the first house we passed and after a short while reappeared carrying an empty pail. Kurt took it from him and turning to Mark shouted an order: "Fill it up. We need water. Go to that pump and fill it up!"

The pump was about twenty feet away. I understood very well how humiliated Mark must feel so I followed intending to help him pump the water.

Kurt called: "Hey you! You stay here."

Soon Mark returned, carrying with both hands the pail full of water. With every step he made, the water splashed around. Both Kurt and Otto screamed with laughter. Kurt pointed at Mark: "This clumsy oaf can't even carry a bucket of water."

"I am an attorney, not a . . ."

"There are no longer Jewish attorneys. You are a swine, that's what you are." Kurt took the pail of water from Mark, raised it up high and, swinging it over Mark's head, poured the water over him.

Mark shivered.

I shivered also.

I pleaded with Kurt to leave my husband alone. In response he roared: "Take a good look at this broad who claims to be the

wife of that clumsy fool who calls himself a man. Not bad, eh?"
Turning to Mark, he snapped: "All right, Jew, you can go. — He's
not worth bothering with anyway."

Water dripping from him, his clothing clinging to his body,
his gold-rimmed glasses in hand, Mark scurried away. When I
started after him, Kurt stopped me. "Not you, you stay here."

Kurt shoved me and Otto pushed Abner toward the pump.

I could sense their effort to invent a scheme that would enter-
tain both themselves and the growing number of onlookers. Kurt
again whispered something into the ear of the Ukrainian. The lat-
ter took the pail, went into the first house,returned with it, and
handed it to me.

"Fill it up," Kurt said.

"Nothing easier," I thought. I placed the pail under the faucet
and pumped. At first the water came slowly. Then in a swift
stream. But the pail did not fill. Kurt screamed at me to fill it up. I
pumped harder. More water poured forth. The pail did not fill.
Kurt laughed, his blue eyes sparkled in delight for his clever joke
had worked perfectly.

He had punched holes in the bottom of the pail.

Tossing back his blonde hair, he stopped laughing and hol-
lered: "I will slowly count to ten and if the bucket is not filled your
laziness will be punished. Remember, the bucket had better be
full!"

It was Abner who had to take the punishment for my "lazi-
ness." He was punched in the abdomen and kicked to the ground.
With his groans in my ears, I bent to my task with more vigor. I
pumped faster, faster, faster. It became a speed marathon that
would perhaps buy the life of my brother. The life he must give in-
stead of Father.

The pumping went on endlessly. I pumped like an automaton,
as if I had never done anything else. then I slipped and fell.

One thought penetrated through the haze in my mind: I must
get up to go on pumping, get up! Get up! Some new strength came
to me when I thought there was none. I tried to reach for the iron
and use it as a support to help me up, but I cut my hand on a sharp
edge and fainted dead away.

I was probably only out for seconds because next I felt
someone grabbing my arm and dragging me directly under the
faucet. "I'll give that dirty Jewess a bath right here," I heard
Kurt's voice distinctly. Cold water streamed over me and revived
me. Through my eyelashes I saw Kurt's blue eyes and they seemed

to express a trace of sympathy as he looked down at me and my bleeding hand.

But I was wrong.

He pushed the handle of the pump down, pulled it up, pushed it down with a fury as if his life depended upon it. No longer sensitive to the water falling on me, I tried to catch my breath and then I heard through the noise made by the squeaking metal pump, Otto's voice: "Let's go, Kurt. These two are finished."

I kept pretending that I had not regained consciousness, opened my eyes only slightly, saw them leave, and did not get up until they were at a safe distance.

Bent with pain, Abner had to make his way to the hut on his own. I could not help him, my own strength was gone.

Though he was in agony I felt that we had to be grateful that Abner's and Mark's lives had not been taken by the Germans instead of Father's.

Sara lovingly attended Abner's bruises. With Lisa in her arms, she crossed the room up and down.

Perele helped me out of my wet clothes and bandaged my hand. Then I slipped into her bed. Resting under covers, I asked, "Where is Mark?"

Instead of fetching him, my stepmother sat down on the edge of her bed. She started to talk softly, sympathetically: "Mark came home as wet as you did. He changed his clothes and left for your apartment. He told me how humiliated he felt and said he would never again be able to face the people in this town. He wouldn't let me squeeze in a word edge-wise. I doubt whether he was fully aware of what he said."

I jumped out of bed, pulled out another dress from the broken wooden closet and hurried to our apartment.

Mark was not there.

From the apartment I went to his office which had been closed since the day the war had started. He was not there either. I knew his exaggerated sense of pride and what a terrible blow it must have been for him to be ridiculed by the same people who only a few weeks back had taken off their hats whenever they crossed his path. But weren't we living in extraordinary times? Should we not accept everything as long as we could remain alive?

I sat down on a chair, thick with dust. The office had a musty, unused odor. I bent my head over the desk and cried.

So immersed was I in my unhappiness that I did not hear

*Blume (Frania) enter the office and come over to me. She handed
me a letter. It read:*

> *My dearest Roma:*
>
> *My love for you and our son is boundless, yet, in spite of
> that, my life in Niemirov is no longer worth living. Since
> your attachment to your family will not permit you to
> leave them, I am compelled to leave you with them. I am
> going to Zlaczov to stay with my parents. I hope you will
> take good care of our son, at least as good as you took of
> your father. We will be together as a family unit as soon
> as circumstances permit. I hope it will be soon . . .*

My attachment to my family . . . I got in touch with Vaclava,
my new landlady in Warsaw. She knew people in the Polish underground who had been planted in the German office that dealt
with the issue of identification cards. A Polish clerk from the
resistance coached Frania on the appropriate answers to all questions on the application form and allowed her to fill out the form,
and fingerprinted her at Vaclava's home. And so she got her *Kennkarte* without ever appearing in the office.

15

"**C**ecylia!" Frania cried. "A Nazi!"

I jumped and peered out of the window.

"That's Rechter," I said. "Go up to the attic, quickly."

Frania ran out of the room and I leaned out of the window, "I'll be right down!" I called. Quickly I went to the mirror and rubbed on some lipstick and smoothed my hair.

"It's beautiful here," Rechter said when I had unlocked the gate.

"That's why I come here whenever I am tired of city living," I said, smiling at him. He was wearing his uniform.

"I hope you don't mind my dropping in," he said.

"Not at all. But this place is not equipped for entertaining — I hope you will forgive me."

"Don't bother about that. Berler mentioned that you were staying here and since you once asked me about a certain Danka Bracka, I came over to give you the information."

I was on guard.

"Danka Bracka belonged to Glasseye's gang and it was she who gave him your address," Rechter said. "She got a share of the loot they took from you."

"What a bitch," I said aloud and it occurred to me that her story about her Jewish fiancé in the Ghetto was a coverup to gain my confidence. And the nights she stayed away from the boarding house were spent with criminals together with whom they planned robberies. "What a bitch," I repeated.

"In a way, I am grateful to her . . ." Rechter said. "Did you know her well?"

"She was employed by Vinetta."

We had slowly walked up the driveway toward the house. Now, standing at the entrance door I was at a loss what to do. I had to give Frania enough time to settle in the attic. Awkwardly I turned about to make him go back to the gate.

"It's a big house," he said. "May I see it?"

I opened the door and said, "The rooms are rather dreary, but you're welcome." I didn't take him to the mouldy-smelling living room downstairs which the carpenters had not yet renovated because I did not want him to see the dilapidated state of the house and begin to suspect my reasons for chosing to live there. I had no alternative but to take him to my room.

He looked around with a certain intensity.

"I like simplicity," I said.

I gestured to the wicker bench.

"Thanks, Miss Szarek, but I have only a few minutes."

"Oh?"

"I'm on duty and there's a train in half an hour." He shook my hand; he did not release it.

"Cecylia, bringing you the information about the Bracka girl was just an excuse."

"An excuse?" I was aware of the beating of my heart and was afraid he would hear it.

"Cecylia, I love you."

Suddenly I was in his arms. Then I stiffened. It was not me he loved. He loved Cecylia Szarek.

"Let go of me!" I cried.

He only held me closer.

"You don't mean that, Cecylia. I could feel a moment ago that you didn't mean that."

"I do. I do. You must believe me," I hesitated, "for your own sake."

"For my sake? What is the matter, Cecylia? Tell me."

"I can't."

"You can tell me anything. Even that you're a member of the Polish underground."

I laughed. I laughed hysterically.

"Don't you understand? I love you. I am not allowed to associate with Polish women. But whatever you are cannot change how I feel."

"*You* don't understand. There is a gulf between us . . ."

"Oh, you don't know how very much I do love you . . ."

I heard his voice with emotion. I trembled. Oh God, how could I love one of them? "There is something terribly wrong with me," I whispered.

"There is nothing wrong with you. You love me, I feel it."

"No!" I protested. "No!"

He drew me closer, his lips touched my eyes, my mouth, and I felt myself sinking. I pushed him away. When he drew me back into his arms, I cried, "I'm a Jew," and I ran to the farthest corner of the room.

He looked at me aghast. "Impossible!" he said.

Did he feel contaminated? Out of his pale lips the word trembled again: "Impossible."

"Impossible that you could fall for a 'subhuman'?" I cried from my corner.

"Stop it."

"Impossible that you could fall for a dirty Jewess?"

"Stop it!"

"My whole family and all the people I love are Jewish. My father was deported because he insisted that my brother save his wife before him. My brother — a Jew, too, of course — went mad at the choice he had to make. That's the kind of family I come from, and that's what you're doing to us!"

"Stop it, stop it!"

"Arrest me. You'll get a second promotion, like after the robbery, for cracking a case . . ."

Rechter's face was white. He tried to interrupt me.

"Impossible, you say? Impossible that the top-notch police investigator, with all his intelligence was duped? What a laugh! I am the 'scum' of the earth, you know. I should be in the Ghetto. But I've got pretensions. I thought I could beat your system . . ." I paused, panting, Then: "Shoot me, why don't you shoot me?"

He took a step toward me — but halted as I went on, not able to stop the flood of invective that poured from me. Exhausted, I slumped against the wall. "Arrest me," I said hoarsely.

"I have no right to make arrests in Konstancin," he answered calmly. His shoulders rigid, he came over to me and out of his tight lips the words were spoken as if by a robot. "I must go now," he said. "I am on duty." He turned woodenly and left slowly, descending in a mechanical fashion as if all life had left him.

I was still standing where he had left me when Frania who,

unheard by me, had slipped into the room, asked: "What happened? I heard you shouting. Did he attack you?"

"Pack!" I said. "They will come for me. I told him I was a Jew."

"I don't believe it."

"Pack and get out of here."

"Let's take only a small case so that we can run if we have to."

"*I* am not going."

"You're crazy."

"I can't show my face anywhere now. You'll have a better chance *alone*."

"Without you I have no chance. Where would I go? Come with me."

"I can't. I am tired. You can go to Julek. You can go to Maria."

"I'm lost without you."

I staggered to the bed and fell on it.

"Go. Please go."

My little sister lay down near me.

Dusk was coming on. From a deep silence Frania's voice chirped in hopefully: "Maybe he isn't going to report you?"

I once again described to her all that had happened between Rechter and me. I talked and cried until I was exhausted, and then I fell asleep.

When Frania woke me it was dark. Trained to be alert at all times, I was immediately on my feet. "They're here, they've come for us," she whispered, and simultaneously I heard steps coming up the stairs.

The end had come. I stroked Frania's hair as we clung together.

Why did it take so long? Why were they so silent? Why didn't they beat down the door?

I could not take the suspense any longer. I switched on the light, dashed to the door and flung it open.

The light, falling into the dark corridor, illuminated a ghostly Rechter.

The next moment I was in his arms. "Poor, poor darling," he whispered. "Poor, poor darling. How could I leave you in such a state of mind?"

He saw Frania, looked at me, and withdrew.

"This is Frania Stanislavska, my best friend," I said. "She knows all about me."

We went and sat on the bed. His eyes caressed me and his hands stroked mine.

Frania poured drinks. Jubilantly, she said, "To both of you." Then she grabbed her sweater and, opening the door to the balcony, she said, "I'll watch the gate."

We waited until she had closed the door and then fell back into each other's arms.

"Forgive me, darling," he said. "You must have gone through hell during these last three hours. but I needed time to think. I want you to know I've always hated being a police investigator. Now I'm grateful for it because I'll be able to protect you. Tonight I just want to hold you for the time I can stay here. Soon I must be on my way. I'm on duty tonight."

He kissed me and stroked me and then he had to go. At the doorway, he turned and said: "I am happy because you trusted me. I'll be back tomorrow evening."

I went to the balcony and, my arm around Frania, watched Rolf walk down the driveway whistling. Suddenly he broke into a run. When he reached the gate, instead of opening it, he climbed up and leapt over to the other side.

16

Next morning on my way to the station, my feet hardly touched the ground. Frania was going to visit Julek at dawn, and tonight I would be alone with Rolf. He would hold me in his arms. How happy I was!

What would Father say? I would tell Rolf what had happened to him. He might know where he had been sent. To me, at that time, Rechter could do anything!

I danced across the platform station, I leapt on to the train. All the way to Warsaw I felt as if I were flying. I treated myself to a rickshaw and, bursting into the Vinetta offices, sang out, "Good morning, everybody." I even kissed Maria.

The translation of a complicated contract became suddenly easy. The awful *Eintopfgericht* at the Gondola tasted delicious. I laughed with the girls about Berler's latest fad, Buddhism, and returned to my cubicle ecstatic, as if drugged.

The telephone rang.

It was Weinstein asking me to come to his office at once.

After my successful intervention at the *Umschlagplatz* Weinstein gave me thick envelopes to be delivered at addresses enroute to BBH offices. These were innumerable messages to and from the Ghetto — by word of mouth or written — and, though I felt that he was sometimes taking advantage of my willingness to help, I couldn't refuse.

Lately Berler had cut my trips to the Ghetto to a minimum. Perhaps the rumors abroad that there were shootings in the streets were true. Mr. Korman's preparations to escape from the Ghetto proved how much life inside had deteriorated. On the pretext of making a merchandise shipment, I succeeded in removing part of his belongings from the Ghetto to the Aryan side.

I went slowly down the stair. In the antique shop I asked for Weinstein and was led to his room.

"*Dzien dobry* (good day), Miss Szarek," Weinstein's greeting was as usual extremely cordial. "Meet Mr. Parczycki," he pointed at a strange man sitting slumped in a chair. He offered me a seat, gave me a cigarette, and said: Mr. Parczycki has a Jewish girl friend in the Ghetto. He wishes to send her ten thousand zlotys to buy a job in a German-run factory. This will protect her against deportation and will give them the hope that they soon may be reunited."

It was obvious to me that Mr. Parczycki was himself a Jew and that his "girlfriend" in the Ghetto was his wife. What they were asking was that I, presumably a Polish woman, should risk my life for them.

"I told you last week, Mr. Weinstein, that it was the last time I would carry a package of yours to the Ghetto. It was dangerous then, and it is dangerous now . . ."

Weinstein, who had been pacing up and down, stopped in front of me and, his black eyes fixed upon mine, said, "I ask you this once. Take the money to her."

"I no longer have a pass."

"You can easily get one."

"If Berler gives me a commission, I'll get a pass and go."

"I already asked him. He refused. I thought you might want to help anyway." He pointed to the stranger whose tears were rolling down his hollow cheeks.

Another face with a glowing red beard appeared before my mind's eye — My father in the Market Place sacrificing his own life so that Abner and Sara could be together.

"Bring me the money," I said.

Parczycki jumped to his feet and took my hand. "God bless you, God bless you," he said.

At the *Transferstelle* where I got a pass the clerk advised me to be on my guard. He told me that the inhabitants of the "small

Ghetto" were moving out into the big Ghetto. "And you know the Jews . . ."

I called Rolf, and made up some story that I had to go to the Ghetto on behalf of Vinetta. I told him what the clerk had said and asked him whether he could accompany me.

At four o'clock in the afternoon at the Ghetto entrance the guard checked my pass and to my surprise asked Rolf as well for his. Casually, Rolf presented his police identification.

"This is not a *Passierschein*," the guard said.

"It should suffice," Rolf said shortly.

The guard said that his order prohibited him from letting even Hitler himself through without a pass. He asked Rolf what he was carrying in the briefcase he had taken out of my hand to carry along the way.

"Nothing," Rolf answered.

The guard asked him to open it, saw a package wrapped in newspaper, tore the wrapping off and the packet of paper bills came into sight. Without a word he ordered us to a nearby shack. He picked up a phone and reported to his superior, a *Sturmband-fuhrer*, that two people had been caught smuggling money into the Ghetto and that one of them was a German.

Shortly thereafter the *Sturmbandfuhrer* drove up in a Mercedes. He interrogated Rolf and then ordered both of us into his car. We were taken to the Criminal Police Headquarters. There he asked for Rolf's superior. When he was told that *Kommissar* Korben had gone home already, he had him summoned back.

He left us standing in the corridor in the custody of a police guard.

Eventually, *Kommissar* Korben arrived. he was a tall broad-shouldered man. Although his features looked oriental it was impossible that he should have been or he would never have held this position. Without as much as a glance at me, he ordered Rolf to follow him to his office. Then I heard him shouting at Rolf.

How could I have involved the man I loved in my disaster? It was only a matter of time for me, but why had I dragged Rolf to the edge of the precipice?

I got up.

The police guard sprang to attention.

"I must speak to the *Kommissar*," I said.

"Sit down and keep quiet!" the guard ordered.

The door adjacent to the *Kommissar's* office opened and a grim Schleger came out. "It doesn't look good," he said to me. "I heard the *Kommissar* scream his head off and saw him through the inner connecting door make Rolf hand over his gun." Then Schleger noticed a peculiar look on the face of the guard and quickly returned where he came from.

Thoughts of how I might be able to help Rolf out of his predicament raced through my aching head. They centered on only one possibility and that was why I had to speak to the *Kommissar* at that moment. But time seemed to stand still. When finally he came out of his office and headed down the corridor, I was beside him with one jump. *"Herr Kommissar"* I appealed to that impassive gaze, "I must speak to you."

"I'm busy now," he snapped. "You'll be called soon enough."

"You must hear me now. Please! Before you take any further steps."

A flicker of curiosity came to his eyes. "I've no time right now. But I'll see you, you can be sure of that!"

I refused to acknowledge the threat in his voice. Running after him, I cried: "You'll be interested to learn what I've got to say: I know you will."

He opened a door and banged it shut in my face.

The guard grabbed me by my arm and pulled me back to the bench.

Suddenly *Kommissar* Korben came out, called me in, and even offered me a seat.

Sitting on the edge of the chair I blurted out: "You must hear the truth. The money found in Rechter's possession is *my* money. With the recent bombardments, I thought it safer to carry it on me. When I went to the Ghetto for Vinetta today I asked Mr. Rechter to come along because I had heard that the situation there was tense. Mr. Rechter, like a gentleman, carried my briefcase. I swear he did not know what was inside until it was opened by the gate guard." I took a breath. "This is the truth, *Herr Kommissar.*" I looked straight into his eyes.

"What's between you two?" he asked quietly.

"We are friends."

"Oh, I see, just friends —?"

"Yes, just friends." He gave me a mocking smile.

"Don't you know that Germans are prohibited from fraternizing with Poles?"

"No," I said.

He pressed a buzzer and Schleger came in. "Stay with her," he said and left the room.

A little later I heard a car engine start in the courtyard. Schleger stepped to the window and looked out. "Korben is leaving," he said. Then he turned. "Rolf is still in Korben's office with Korben's deputy, Mr. Kruger. It looks bad for Rolf."

We stared at one another. My heart was beating terribly. "I must make a call," I said.

Schleger looked at me aghast. "Impossible!"

"It is for Rolf," I said. "If anybody comes, you throw yourself on me as if I had just grabbed the phone." Without waiting for Schleger's answer I reached for the phone and gave Zosia's number to the switchboard operator. I heard the ring and then Zosia's "Hello."

"Listen Zosia. Listen carefully. I went to the Ghetto this morning on Vinetta business. Rolf was with me. There was some misunderstanding and we were arrested. Get in touch with Berler."

Schleger said, "Enough, enough!"

I hung up. Had Zosia understood? Would Berler stick his neck out for us? If not, I would be caught lying and Korben would know that we had tried to smuggle money into the Ghetto.

We sat waiting in silence. Schleger offered me a cigarette.

About eleven o'clock, Korben returned. He dismissed Schleger and buzzed for Kruger. He was lighting a cigar when his deputy came in and, still on the threshold asked, "How did it go, Chief?"

"I did it." The *Kommissar* said, grinning with satisfaction. This S.S. man is a hard nut to crack, but you know *me.* He won't have my men pulled into such quagmire. Not my men!"

His black eyes twinkled and his inscrutable face beamed.

Kruger, shaking his superior's hand, said emphatically: "Great! Really great, Chief."

"As for this one —" Korben turned to squint at me and, puffing on his cigar, said: "Miss Szarek, I must insist that you never see Rechter again. I want your promise."

"Why?"

"It is against the law to fraternize with Poles," he said. "You will not answer any of his letters and you will give instructions at home and at the office that you are not available should he call. I advise you to stick to these orders. And here is your money." The newspaper wrapped package dropped into my lap. "Count it. Kruger, you are a witness. I won't have the honesty of the German police doubted."

"I don't care about my money," I cried. "But *Herr* Rechter's friendship is precious to me." I put the package on the desk.

"You don't understand, Miss Szarek, this promise is the condition for your release. The money is not a bargaining point."

"I don't want to be released on such a condition."

"Not only does *your* release depend on it, but Rechter's release depends on it too."

He had me where he wanted me. I bowed my head.

"Now, count the money. Kruger, have her sign a receipt."

I signed the receipt and Kruger gave me a pass which allowed me to go home after curfew. He took me down the stairs to the main exit door and said, "Sorry, Miss Szarek . . ."

Outside, I glanced back at the Criminal Police Headquarters and then at the barred windows of the prison cells.

Once again I had come through a tight situation.

I breathed the night air in deeply, exhaled, and breathed in again. Just for the fun of it.

I started to walk briskly just for the pleasure of feeling my limbs move. I took a wrong turning and didn't care — and walked on at random and suddenly flung my arms open wide, wishing I could embrace the whole city. I would find a way to see Rolf secretly. But then tears sprang to my eyes. I wiped them off and walked on.

All at once I was aware that I was being followed. I did not look back. I realized I might be picked up and arrested again. People were always picked up on the slightest pretext.

A church materialized in the darkness. I hurried toward it but its doors were locked. I dropped to my knees and prayed to the God of all men for endurance, and that I might be permitted to live a little longer.

17

The hollow footsteps behind me kept coming closer. I crouched near to the stone wall and hugged it shivering. In a few more moments I would be at the mercy of the person who was following me. The muffled figure passed in the darkness and the sound of the steps slowly faded away.

I stood up. The safest place for me would be Konstancin where I was not police registered. But at this time of night it was impossible to get there so I had to take the risk and go to Vaclava's, my "legal home."

Everything was exactly as I had left it a few days before when I had come to get some warm clothing for Konstancin. Korben had not searched my room.

As I started to undress the telephone rang in the hallway. At this hour it had to be for me. The person who had been following me had lost me on the way and now he was checking on me. If I didn't answer another boarder would.

I ran to the hallway. My voice was quivering when I said, "Hello —"

"May I speak to *Fraulein* Szarek?"

"Who's calling?"

"Schleger is my name —."

"It's me, Mr. Schleger."

"Thank God. Rolf is out of his mind with worry. I couldn't inform him what happened to you after Korben dismissed me."

I took a deep breath.

Then I heard Rolf's voice: "I'm the happiest man alive. You're safe my darling."

"And *you,* Rolf?"

"I'm fine, just fine."

"Rolf, I had to give my word to your boss, not to see you again. Not even to speak to you over the phone. I *had* to."

"I had to swear not to see you too. Korben and Kruger forced me to."

"Don't mention names over the phone."

"I won't keep my promise."

"But it was an order. They'll find out."

"All I know is that I'm not giving you up. If I have to pay for my happiness, I'll pay. Even if it's two years in a concentration camp —"

"I won't let you ruin your life."

"They can't do that to us."

"That is just what they can do . . ."

"*Ich pfeife auf sie* (damn them)! If they're listening, I want them to know I care more for you than for the whole damn war!" Then there was silence as if he himself was aghast at the vehemence of his own words and what consequences they could bring.

Frania had taken a room in Konstancin. She had found a dressmaker who told her of a neighbor, a gardener by the name of Antony, who was looking for a tenant.

The room was tiny, in a gatehouse occupied by a family of five on the grounds of a large estate. A luxurious villa, equipped with all modern facilities, two hundred feet away, was empty, its Jewish owner, Wirtman, gone. Frania had registered with the Konstancin police and, once she had the correct identification papers, promptly had gone to Warsaw to look for another room so as to have two places, in case of an emergency. She had rented a room on Creditova Street not far from Vinetta, and had found work she could do at home, crocheting and knitting dresses.

I was so occupied with Frania that I was able somehow to half-block Rolf out of my mind. Two weeks had passed since that dreadful day. He had called regularly at Vinetta, pleading with me to see him after work. But I had put him off with various excuses. It became more and more difficult, especially in the presence of my co-workers whose sympathies were all on his side. I could feel my resistence wearing thin, and decided to ask *Kommissar* Korben to free us from our pledge. I wrote the draft of a letter.

> *Sehr geehrter Herr Kommissar:*
> Wasn't there one among all the paintings you have seen in your life that said more to you than all the others?
> Of all the concerts you have heard, wasn't there one that gripped you more than the rest?
> And of all the landscapes you have known, hasn't there been one where you felt most at home?
> Rolf Rechter and I feel that we have found in each other that one painting that holds us spellbound, that one concert that keeps reverberating in us, and the landscape to which we belong.
> We have not seen each other during these two weeks. We have kept our promise. But already it is becoming unbearable, and I feel myself faltering. Since you told me that breaking my word would bring harm to him, I know only one way out: To ask you, *Herr Kommissar,* to please release us from our pledges. Amidst all the brutality of war, permit, I beg you — one thing of beauty to survive!
> *Hochachtungsvoll.*
> Cecylia Szarek

I put the letter aside to review it at some later moment. However, another telephone call from Rolf made me so desperate to see him that I was driven to take immediate action.

I went to the Police Headquarters and asked to see Mr. Kruger.

"I need your advice," I told him. First I let him read the letter to the *Kommissar* and then I asked whether he thought I should mail it.

"What can you lose?" Kruger asked.

Just as I was about to leave Korben entered. Kruger, a little disconcerted at having been caught in a private conversation with a Pole, said that I was waiting to see him.

I was in trouble.

Korben invited me to his office and, having no choice, I handed him the letter.

He read and reread it, his oriental features showing no expres-

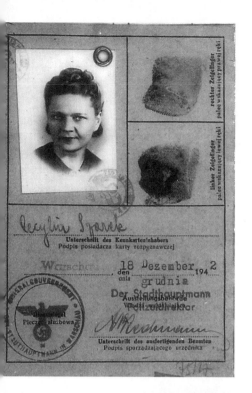

Identity card issued to Sandra Brand as Cecylia Szarek

Bescheinigung
Poświadczenie

§ 3 Abs. 5 der Ersten Durchführungs-
vorschrift zur Verordnung über die Einführung einer Arbeitskarte vom 21.12.1940

§ 3 ust. 5 pierwszego postanowienia wy-
konawczego do rozporządzenia o wpro-
wadzeniu karty pracy z dnia 21.XII.1940

Name:
Nazwisko *Szarek*

Vorname:
Imię *Cecylia*

Geboren am:
Urodzony(a) dnia *6. September 1913*

Geburtsort:
Miejsce urodz. *Bratkówka*

Kreis:
Powiat *Krosno*

Beruf *Verkäuferin.*
Zawód *Sprzedawczyni.*

Berufsgruppe und Art *25a 2.*
Grupa zawod.

ist auf Grund der Verordnung
über die Einführung einer Arbeitskarte vom 20. 12. 1940 als
arbeitskartenpflichtige Person
erfasst und ist im Besitze der Arbeitskarte
Nr.: 919/203321

zarejestrowany został na podsta-
wie rozporządzenia o wprowadze-
niu karty pracy z d. 20. 12. 1940
jako osoba, zobowiązana do po-
siadania karty pracy i posiada
kartę pracy
Nr.: ...

Warschau, den *20. Juni* 194*2*

(Stempel des Arbeitsamts)
(pieczęć Urzędu Pracy)

Dienstsiegel
Pieczęć
służbowa

ARBEITSAMT-WARSCHAU

Arbeitsamt Warschau
im Auftrage

(Unterschrift — Podpis)

Diese Bescheinigung verbleibt im Besitz des Inhabers
Niniejsze zaświadczenie pozostaje w posiadaniu posiadacza karty.

Abk. 1. Din A6.   Staatsdruckerei Warschau — Nr. 96607-42.

Work permit issued to Sandra Brand as Cecylia Szarek.

sion. Then he looked at me for a long moment, after which he stood up and left the office.

I heard him roar frighteningly in the corridor. He'll kill me for this letter, I thought.

Then the door opened. I could not believe my eyes.

It was Rolf.

"Cecylia, you?" He was just as surprised as I. "The *Kommissar* said there was a phone call." He gave me a brilliant smile. "It's really you," he said, and took me in his arms, and held me tightly against him.

Korben gave Rolf the afternoon off. As we were leaving the *Kommissar* shook a threatening finger at us. "You youngsters, be careful now. If they ever catch you again —"

As we passed his deputy's room on the way out we saw him give us a wide, happy smile.

On the train to Konstancin, however, we kept up appearances but the silence between us was heavy with a lovely tension.

I had to repress my longing to touch his hand, his hair, his cheeks, because I feared the Polish passenger's disdain. But once in the woods we walked with our arms wrapped around each other.

Rolf kicked pebbles out of my path and bent low hanging branches out of my way. The path leading to villa June was no longer peopled by ghosts.

Silently we climbed the dim stairway.

Inside my room Rolf took the key out of my hand, inserted it into the keyhole and turned it twice.

"I love you, Cecylia," he said, and his body pressed against mine for the first time. "I love you more than my life, and I feel you love me too, my darling woman, even though you cannot bring yourself to say it."

18

Rolf made me promise to let him know every time I left my home or my office; what night I would spend at Vaclava's and what train I might take to Konstancin. If I were arrested, he could then attempt to get my release without delay. Only if the Gestapo were involved, might he possibly be powerless.

I did not always keep my promise. I did not tell him of my dealings with Weinstein.

Weinstein had borrowed my Ghetto pass for his sister, who wanted to use it to escape from the Ghetto to the Aryan side. Two days later, a stranger called me over the phone, mentioned Weinstein's name, and asked me to meet her at Belveder Station.

Malvina, who was about my age, returned my pass to me at the station and confided to me that she was not Weinstein's sister but a refugee he was helping. Tomorrow she would get in touch with a helpful non-Jewish friend but tonight she had no place to sleep.

I could not bring her to Vaclava's. Vaclava might become suspicious. I had to break an appointment with Rolf in order to take her to Konstancin.

Malvina did not contact her non-Jewish friend the next day nor the following days, preferring to stay in villa June. For a whole week I avoided Rolf because I had to carry food to Malvina. We slept together in my bed until I told her that she was no longer welcome. Then Weinstein asked me to lend him my pass again and again until it became a four day routine.

Although sharing my bed with unkempt strangers was certainly no pleasure to me, my life, I felt, had taken on a purpose higher than merely my own survival. Smelling the sweat of Malvinas, Bertas, Friedas and Reginas, became a regular part of it. Most of them were bigger and taller than I and, unlike Frania who used to curl up against the wall, they had a tendency to push me to the edge of the bed. It was difficult to get rid of them because they felt safe in the villa June hideout.

No wonder that Weinstein urged me to have them move on as quickly as possible since other "relatives" were waiting their turn and it meant instant death for anyone stealing out of the Ghetto without proper papers. Although I was exhausted most of the time and wanted to be left alone, nevertheless, when a few days passed with no fugitive in sight, I became restless and waited anxiously for Weinstein to call on me.

At times the scheming and the running became too much for me. Stories of my fame in the Ghetto — my nickname became *the goldene Shikse* — gave me little consolation. One thing disturbed me particularly.

My ritual of looking at the piece of photograph of Bruno before going to bed had to be given up for I had to be on my guard at all times in front of these Jewish girls as well as in front of non-Jews. These precious moments of intimacy with my child had many times to be given up. Recently, instead of coming to me in my dreams, my child had appeared while I was eating. Pale, skinny, with no shine in his flaxen hair, he wobbled on spike-like legs and stared with terrible intensity at my plate.

Was my child starving? Was he being maltreated? Did he reproach me?

Did he reproach me? I saw his slender body cuddled on his grandfather's lap, watching him with round eyes, as he was singing Zmirous *(table hymns). It was Friday night at the dinner table. Father had come home from his hideout in Radroz, a day after the Germans had left for the agreed-upon demaracation line at the River San. Only for me and Bruno was the pleasure of our reunion clouded.*

"You haven't heard from Mark, have you?" Father asked.

Bruno turned to me and stared at me. Was he reproaching me? "No, I haven't."

The lights of the six candles in the silver candlesticks on the table flickered.

"You'll hear from him soon," Father said, and his face again radiated happiness and serenity as it had a minute ago. "Thank God for that," he added.

"It isn't over yet," Abner said. "Another few days and the Russians will be here. Who knows how the Communists will treat us."

Father's smile disappeared for a second but his words sounded confident and prophetic as well: "The Russians may cause us some hardship but never like the Germans. Anyway, God's ways are unknown to us mortals. May His will be our law."

The thought suddenly flashed through my mind: Of the two men, Mark and my father, the latter was by far the stronger. Living by the rules of the Torah, he had found an equilibrium. He demanded little of life and accepted if less came his way.

Mark was as determined as Father. However, his goal was to be accepted by the Gentiles. In his opinion the attitude of the Hassidim and the Orthodox was the main reason for anti-Semitism. By repudiating everything that marked Jewishness he expected to win over the non-Jews. But his whole position broke down, unable to withstand the first storm, when circumstances forced him to face his Jewishness. He ran away from me, the witness to the collapse of his philosophy.

The thought that he might need my help more than Father made me long to comfort him.

I forced a smile, approached Father and took Bruno out of his arms into mine. Holding Bruno close I whispered into his ear: "Baby, as soon as the buses run again, I'll bring your daddy home."

Rolf had access to people under arrest or held in jail for investigation, and sometimes even to those who were detained in the Paviak Prison as political "criminals." All he had to do was to accuse the political prisoner of an ordinary crime and he would be able to get special permission to interrogate him. During that interrogation, he had the opportunity to instruct the accused as to how to prove his innocence or how to gather new evidence for an alibi.

But Rolf took that risk only in cases where death was imminent.

It was easier for him to deal with cases coming into the Criminal Headquarters. Some cases came to his desk in the natural course of events. As for the others, he could intervene with his colleagues. Innumerable people were freed on account of his interventions. There were also other situations to which he gave his attention.

For some time Schone had been paying monthly hush money to two unemployed Poles who had created a lucrative business out of blackmailing Jewish suspects. The money Schone had brought from Cracow had all gone to the extortionists. Now he suspected they were going to denounce him for the reward, as they had done to other victims. "I planned to move to another city," he had said to me, "but how far would I go with this nose?"

I told Rolf about Schone, "The Protestant," having difficulty with two Polish hoodlums because of the shape of his nose. I said he was invovled in underground activities and therefore did not want to come to headquarters to file a complaint.

I told Rolf the date and the time of the hoodlums' next visit. The blackmailers were so sure of Schone that they had the audacity to come to the Vinetta offices for their "stipend."

Rolf showed up in uniform and ordered everybody to produce their *Arbeitskarten* (work cards). Since the two bandits had none, he delivered them to the *Arbeitsamt* (Employment Office) who sent them off to Germany. There they would have to work in ammunition factories, sometimes exposed to bombing.

Shortly after, Mrs. Schone needed help. Her landlady made it clear that she suspected her, and Mrs. Schone decided to move to new quarters. However, her landlady would not permit her to take any of her belongings.

Rolf, in his uniform, went to see Mrs. Schone. The landlady's attitude immediately changed. She asked Mrs. Schone to please remain and even offered a reduction in the rent. Mrs. Schone moved anyway taking all her belongings along while Rolf looked on.

The thoroughness and cruelty with which the Germans carried out their orders left no room for belief in exceptions amongst them. That is why the fact that Rolf repeatedly risked his freedom — and in some cases his life — was a phenomenon we all wondered about.

Maria's cousin, we later found it was her brother, had been arrested. He was accused of some misdemeanor concering postal affairs. Maria claimed he was innocent, but that hardly mattered. Once in the clutches of the police it would soon come to light that he was a disguised Jew.

Rolf found out that he was being held at the Criminal Police Headquarters, arranged to get jursidiction over the case and had him released.

The following weeks and months brought an army of petitioners to my room at Vaclava's. Friends, colleagues, acquaintances — the circle widened. I related the requests to Rolf but he never seemed to grow weary of it all.

"These problems belong to the nation who created them and I share the responsibility," he said one evening. "I can't believe what my countrymen did. I've tried to rationalize. I told myself that certain means were justified if we wanted to fulfill our great destiny as a nation, but from the day I started to work for the police I have seen nothing but evil — evil spreading, like a plague let loose . . ."

Rolf became a key personality in our world. Only God was placed higher. — And I was "God's" acknowledged messenger.

19

Over the phone, Frania asked in a frightened voice if I could come to Creditova Street immediately. I told Zosia that I would be back soon and left the office.

Frania had arrived in Warsaw the day before to deliver two sweaters and had bought a fresh supply of yarn. Then she had returned to Konstancin. But on her way from the station to the Antonys' she had met her dressmaker who told her that the police had been in Antony's gatehouse searching for a hidden Jewess, and that Mrs. Antony had already told her neighbors that the girl going by the name Frania Stanislavska must be the Jewish girl the Germans were after.

"Naturally, I waited a little until the dressmaker had gone, turned around and came back to Warsaw. Now I'm afraid the Antonys are going to send the police after me in Warsaw."

"Did you leave your Warsaw address with them?"

"I'm not that stupid! Of course I didn't."

"Then how can they send the police?"

"You're right. I'm so scared, I can't think straight."

I called my office that I wasn't feeling well and then I called Rolf.

Rolf came over and after learning what had happened he said that Frania had to go back to the Antonys. "If she doesn't they will be able to denounce her when they run into her."

I was surprised. Had he guessed Frania was Jewish? I had never told him.

87

"I'm afraid," Frania said, and she began to cry.

I put my hand on her shoulder and said softly, "Rolf and I will go with you."

Rolf agreed. "All three of us will go." He turned to Frania. "But you will have to stand up to your landlady by yourself and let all hell loose for spreading gossip about you."

"I can't," Frania said.

"You have to," Rolf said. "Shout at her. Tell her malicious gossip like that could land you in a concentration camp before you had the chance to prove your origin. Tell her you'll file a complaint against her for slander."

"I can't do it." She looked at me in entreaty, tears streaming down her cheeks.

Rolf turned to me. "She's got to do it. It's the only way to convince Mrs. Antony. It would never occur to her that a Jew would dare to charge a Gentile."

"What if the Germans come again while I'm there?" Frania sobbed.

"They'll not come again. I know the procedure. Somebody gives them a lead. They search, and if they don't find the Jew they leave it at that, knowing that he'll be tripped up on some other occasion. They're much too busy to take too much trouble over *one* Jew. In any case, we'll be outside watching the road. Once you've made your scene, we'll show up as though we had come visiting."

We set out for Konstancin. Once there, Rolf and I took cover behind an oak tree at a little distance from the Antonys' gatehouse. We heard the dog bark when Frania opened the gate.

It was then that I confessed that Frania was my sister.

"Impossible!" he said. "Both of you are so different."

"She is my sister! And I don't know how to say it, Rolf, I don't know whether you'll understand it, but her survival is more important to me than my own."

Rolf stared down at me. I went on: "We were six children and, strangely enough, we all looked different. She's the youngest. My parents loved her very much and I promised — She must stay alive no matter what the cost."

Rolf stroked my cheek. "I'll remember that," he said. "Now — let's go in."

The dog came to the fence barking at us. Then Frania came through the entrance doorway. She was smiling.

I was radiant for twenty-four hours. Then I learned that my

friend Kovalski was dead. Only three days ago Maria had told me about the villa she and Kovalski had rented in Konstancin, its main feature being that it had many exits should the enemy be seen approaching. Searching out such sites had become our obsessive preoccupation, as if immunity could be won by these means.

Once when Berler was facing one of his many financial squeezes, Kovalski had helped him with a considerable loan so, when Berler heard that Kovalski was moving, he offered him the use of an otherwise unobtainable removal van.

Maria had seated herself in the closed front-cab next to the driver while Kovalski sat in the back in order to watch their suitcases. At the outskirts of Warsaw two Polish plainclothesmen stopped them. Kovalski was ordered to climb down, go into the nearest apartment building and, in the shadows behind the stairs, drop his trousers.

Maria terrified at the exposure of the fact that her friend was a Jew, had slipped her wrist-watch into the driver's hand, pushed the cab door open and run in the opposite direction. When she heard shots, she turned her head and saw Kovalski running out of the building and then drop to the pavement.

Now Maria sat in Zosia's living room, staring straight ahead. Zosia said that she had been sitting like that for a long time. I went over and I took her hand and stroked it.

"I like lavender," Maria said.

What did she mean?

"Cecylia, if you buy a new cake of soap use it gently, it might be him." And she, who seldom smiled, laughed out loud.

Zosia who was in the kitchen preparing dinner could not have heard Maria's reference to soap, but I worried whether, in her state of mind, Maria might not say something that would make Zosia wonder. I went into the kitchen and said, "Maria is in a state of shock."

"Is she Jewish, too?" Zosia asked bluntly.

"It never occurred to me," I said.

"I don't know how you feel about these matters but, you see, I happen to like her. I want her to stay with me until the police give up looking for her. There's a spare bed in the bedroom but she's insisted on the living room couch. Is she afraid I'll find out she's Jewish when she gets undressed?"

"What could you *see*?"

"You don't know?" Zosia asked surprised. "Everyone does.

Jews are different. Men are circumcised and the female organ is horizontal instead of vertical."

I laughed.

"Didn't you know?"

"Of course," I said. "I'm laughing because of your face — Go and look at it,"

Zosia stepped up to the wall mirror and laughed herself. "I've been peeling beets," she said. "I'm making borsht."

When I returned to the living room Maria said: "I must see Rolf."

"He can't do anything for Kovalski, and you're safe here," I said.

"I must see him!" she repeated.

When Rolf came to see Maria next evening she asked him to help her regain Kovalski's belongings.

I told her that each of Rolf's interventions was a great risk to him and that he should take risks for *people's lives* and not their possessions. But Maria was so insistent that Rolf promised to try.

Later, when he had gone, she confided to me why she had insisted on getting back Kovalski's belongings. His diamonds were sewn into the seams of his bathrobe. The jewels, she felt, belonged to her. What she didn't consider was that her greed might endanger Rolf.

Rolf informed the Polish police that the requisitioned property had been Berler's and that Kovalski, who had been employed by him, had been carrying out his employer's orders in bringing them over to villa Vera in Konstancin.

Because the Polish police were subserviant to the German police and a German was claiming the property, the suitcases were promptly delivered to Berler's villa and Berler gave them to Maria.

Along the way, the diamonds disappeared.

20

From the time Frania had found a place of her own, I no longer had to commute to Konstancin, unless I had to carry food to a girl hidden in villa June.

Most of the time Rolf and I met in Vaclava's and we spent only an occasional few hours on weekends in villa June. Vaclava, her parents, and her two brothers liked Rolf and received him warmly.

One day, coming home from work, I saw Rolf and Vaclava's oldest brother, Bronislav, with their heads together in earnest conversation. Bronislav knew enough German to make himself understood.

"What weighty problems are you two trying to solve?" I asked jokingly.

They looked at me guiltily. Before I had a chance to ask anything further the air raid sirens howled. Usually I stayed in my room during an air raid because I feared the scrutinizing glances of the other tenants in the cellar more than the possiblity of being killed by a bomb. But this time Rolf forced me to go to the cellar.

When we entered all eyes turned to Rolf. No doubt the Poles resented that I had brought a Geman, but at least they would not suspect me of being a Jew.

Rolf rolled a barrel into an empty corner and helped me up. I sat down and after a time took out my precious bit of photograph. "Is there sòmebody taking care of you, my darling?" I murmured. "Rolf has searched for you in camps like Treblinka and, thank

God — your name was not registered. I will find you, I promise. The time will come when I will find you!"

Rolf was by now used to hearing me talk to myself in this fashion. I put the piece of photograph back into an envelope and put the envelope into my pigskin pocketbook. We sat listening to the roar of the bombers overhead and the deafening explosions. The brick wall behind us trembled and we locked our hands under my green scarf.

"Afraid?" Rolf asked.

"No," I said. I was not afraid of a "normal" death. If it should come it would not be because I had been singled out; it would hit whoever was in the cellar whether Jew, Pole, or German.

There was an exceptionally loud noise of an exploding bomb. Rolf threw me to the floor and himself on top of me. The ground shook.

"That was a close one," he whispered into my ear.

When the all-clear sounded and we filed out of the shelter I took his arm for everyone to see.

Because of the frequent bombings Rolf insisted that I spend nights in Konstancin even though it meant commuting again, and seeing each other less often.

The grounds of villa June were at their most beautiful in October. On the balcony in the dark, I inhaled the scent of pine, and listened to the soft rustle of the foliage and imagined it was Bruno's chatter. And as I watched the glow of the fireflies, I thought how Rolf's love had brightened my life.

I heard a soft whistle. There it was again, making my heart beat faster.

"Cecylia!"

I flew down the stairs and into his arms. "How did you come here? There are no trains this late."

"A colleague brought me out here. I had to see you. Let's go upstairs."

"What's wrong?" I asked when we were sitting side by side on the wicker bench.

He took both of my hands and said: "I'm being sent to Russia. Witebsk. I'm leaving in the morning."

I stared at him speechless.

"I've been assigned as a temporary replacement for a man who has mysteriously disappeared. As soon as Berlin sends a regular replacement I'll be back. By Christmas for sure. Don't cry, darling. I'll be back. It's only for a few weeks."

"Why did they pick you?"

"I don't know . . ."

"You said that *Kommissar* Korben complained of being understaffed."

"I was appointed by the Gestapo."

They want to separate us!"

"Possibly. But I'll be back soon," he said, and he held me close.

"I hope nothing happens in the meantime," I murmured.

"I've made arrangements with Kruger and Schleger, they're my friends. They'll stand by you. But don't turn to them for help where anything to do with your being Jewish is involved. They don't know you're a Jew. You must not admit it to them or to anyone, even under torture! Promise!"

"I promise," I whispered.

"Schleger has the key to my room. I've told him to sell any of my things including the accordion, if you should need money."

"The accordion, never!"

"Silly darling. I can get another instrument . . ."

"What does 'mysterious disappearance' mean?" I asked. My lips were trembling.

"You mean that fellow in Witebsk? He might have done something stupid. But I will watch my step, don't worry."

"I do worry."

"Darling," he kissed me, "Will you wait for me?"

I could no longer speak.

The rest of the night was filled with caresses, tears, dozing off, and fearful awakenings.

It seemed that he had only just arrived when the light of early dawn began to show at the edge of the windows' paper shades.

He stood beside the bed in his uniform. "Good bye, my darling," he said.

The door closed. I was alone.

Then he was back. "I love you, Ceclia, I'll never give you up."

Again the door shut and again he was back for one more embrace, one more look, and one more time to cradle my face in his hands.

And then he was gone.

The next afternoon Rolf called the office to tell me that his departure had been delayed because the train had to wait for an engine. He was not allowed to leave his quarters but he would try to call again.

Each time the telephone rang, I waited to hear his voice. My colleagues were sad, too, and their sympathy for me made me feel that Rolf was lost already. I recalled Vaclava once saying that a mission to Russia was equal to a death sentence. She knew more than the others since her brother Bronislav held a high position in the *Armja Krajowa* (Polish underground).

Then Rolf called again. He said he might be able to see me once more before the train finally left. Two days later at noon, when everyone was out for lunch, he came bursting into my office, took me into his arms, and whirled me around. "Isn't it beautiful? Isn't fate good to us? We're together again!"

"Have they let you off going?"

"No. But we must be grateful for small blessings. Mustn't we?" He handed me a folder containing some music sheets on which he had written a composition signed Robrand. "I chose this pseudonym to keep your real name alive," he whispered.

"I wanted to tell him at long last how much I loved him, but I only could put my arms around him and say nothing.

"Wait until you see the rest." He let me go and dashed into the hallway, coming back with a package. "Happy name day."

According to the Roman calendar, November 22nd was Saint Cecylia day. My co-workers had been holding whispering conferences for some time which they had always halted upon seeing me. But I soon gathered that they were preparing a surprise party at Zosia's. Since Rolf would be in Witebsk by then he had brought his present now — a handbag made of crocodile skin.

After this short visit to the office he kept in touch by telephone during the following five days. Then his calls ceased.

Only now when I could not hear his voice — even if it were only over the phone — did I realize how terrible this separation was going to be. I tried, through Maria, to have the party canceled, but Zosia would not hear of it.

On November 22nd at five o'clock I showed up at Zosia's. The living room was decorated with gladiolae and the table lavishly set. Zosia handed me a bouquet of long stemmed red roses. "From Rolf," she said.

At first I was touched by the fuss made over me but then I became depressed. Some of the people who had spent time and effort and money to arrange this party would callously send me to my death if they ever learned the truth.

I know how you feel, Maria said with her eyes. She embraced me and whispered in my ear: "It's part of the game and we'd better play it well . . ."

Berler demonstrated an experiment in telepathy and an opera singer hired for the occasion, sang, *"Smiej sie Pajaco . . ."* (an aria from the opera Pagliacci).

When the singer stopped, tears which I had managed to keep down welled up in my eyes.

"All of us miss him," Vaclava said, her hand on my shoulder. "Even Bronislav. He lost — he lost a friend."

"Smile, Cecylia, you'll see Rolf sooner than you think," Zosia cried, with a mischievious intonation in her voice.

Schleger turned on a radio he had brought along. But even this treat — Poles were forbidden to own radios — was of no avail. Despite my struggle, perhaps because I had had too much vodka, tears rolled down my face.

Everybody was looking at me. Why those knowing smiles?

I seemed to see Rolf in the hallway and stopped breathing as if by that alone I could maintain this mirage of Rolf making his way toward me. Then I closed my eyes. I felt his embrace, and his face against mine. I opened my eyes.

It was Rolf!

I held him tightly and cried and laughed and heard the others laughing as if they were very far away. I wanted to hear only Rolf; I had only eyes for him.

He had come to say a final good-bye before leaving for Witebsk.

Although I had no permit to be on the street after curfew I took the risk, and Rolf and I went to my room at Vaclava's.

The days and weeks passed slowly. Once in a while Schleger handed me a short note from Rolf. The one real letter was given to me by a soldier on furlough. It was clear that Rolf was afraid to use the normal mail routes. In this letter he told me that the replacement had arrived from Berlin, but there was so much confusion at Witebsk that everybody avoided the responsibility of issuing orders for his return to Warsaw. He had written to *Kommissar* Korben asking him to put in a request for him but so far had heard nothing.

I had the crazy idea of going to Police Headquarters to find out whether anything had been done. I did not dare go directly to the *Kommissar;* my courage reached only as far as asking for Kruger. It was from him that I learned that Rolf had been sent to Russia by the Gestapo as a disciplinary measure and that, therefore, the *Kommissar* could be of no help.

"Why?" I asked.

"Well . . ."

"Herr Kruger, please —"

"For having an illicit relationship with a Pole —"

"Somebody talked."

"We believe it was *Sturmbandfuhrer* Holle."

"But he promised to leave our arrest at the Ghetto unreported. Remember *Kommissar* Korben boasted . . . I mean, said . . . Besides, it was such a long time ago."

Kruger shrugged his shoulders. "Who knows?" he said.

As I was about to leave, Schleger handed me seven letters from Rolf. By not writing directly to me he proved that he knew or at least had an inkling as to why he had been sent to Russia. I put the letters unopened into my pocketbook to read them later in the quiet of villa June. The thrill of anticipation throughout the rest of the day dulled my gloom.

But the letters only made me more anxious. In each Rolf promised a different date for his return but those dates had already passed and his words of hope were painful to read. It was very hard to have to accept that Rolf was far away, in Russia.

In 1939 the first heavy Soviet tanks came rolling in to Niemirov from the east, from Rava-Ruska.

As I promised Bruno, I made a special trip to Zloczov to find my husband. My sister-in-law Suzan, who was twenty-three years older than I, opened the door. Although her blonde hair was in curlers, she showed no discomfiture at seeing me.

"Where is Mark?" I asked, and held my breath.

"He's out."

"How is he?"

"He's all right. But isn't your concern a little late? Couldn't you have come looking for him rather sooner instead of staying home with your family?"

"I had to wait until the buses ran again."

"How is Bruno?" she asked, in a softer voice.

"He's fine."

When Mark came home I ran and threw myself into his arms.

He seemed quite taken aback and I saw him glance quickly at Suzan. I felt myself begin to blush. It humiliated me that he could never show affection for me in front of her.

"If only you could see Bruno," I said as soon as we were in his room. "Don't you love us at all, Mark?"

"Of course I do. I love you and I love Bruno," he said in a self-righteous voice, and he glanced at the door in the direction of his sister's room.

"I intend to move to Lvov, where neither of our families will interfere in our life. What do you think, Mark?"

"As soon as you'll be in Lvov, I'll join you."

Then, abruptly, he began to make love to me.

Next morning, I lingered in bed as long as I thought it would not offend Suzan. Then I dressed and came to the breakfast table in the dining room.

"Coffee or milk?" Suzan asked.

"Milk, please," I said but then, remembering her frequent comments about my childishness, I changed my mind and said: "No, I'll have a cup of coffee, please."

Suzan went through the folding door to the kitchen and came back with the coffeepot.

Without thinking, I dropped three cubes of sugar into the brown liquid she poured into my cup.

"When will you grow up, little girl? You still like sweets more than anything else." Suzan said coldly.

I pretended not to have heard. When a crumb of bread caught in my throat and I coughed, she turned to Mark and said: "Her table manners are terrible."

I covered my mouth with the damask napkin and looked imploringly at Mark. He puffed on his pipe and stared into his cup of coffee.

21

few of the Vinetta employees, Maria and I among them, were transferred to a metal plant that Berler had bought up. Although Berler made out that it was a promotion I soon realized it was the opposite but I didn't care. What did interest me was the fact that the building, with its many nooks, crannies, and exits, was ideally suited for hiding or escaping.

Once Maria and I were making an inventory and were far away enough from the other workers for her to ask me whether I would resume my Jewish name after the war.

"At first I hated the name Cecylia Szarek," I said. "But by now I've decided to remain Cecylia Szarek forever. It's been much easier for the Szareks than it's been for the Brands. I'll go to Zloczov and fetch Bruno and then I'll emigrate."

"I could never leave Poland."

"Oh, I thought so too, once, but now I want to leave Poland forever."

"Where will you go?"

"America."

"Do you have relatives there?"

"No. But I once read a biography of Abraham Lincoln, the American President, and it impressed me. I want my son to become an American."

"The fantasies you have! What will you do in America? It's a foreign country, they speak a different language, how will you feed your child? Anyway, what about Rolf?"

"He wants to work for some World Peace Organization. He says there is one already forming, and its headquarters will be in Switzerland."

Maria laughed, brushing all this aside with a gesture of her hand. Then she said, "By the way, Cecylia, what are we going to do about Christmas?"

The approaching holiday put us in a predicament. Most of our co-workers were going to leave the city to spend Christmas with their families. It was taken for granted that we were going to do the same.

"I guess we'll have to think of something," I said. If worse comes to worst, I'll break a leg, and you'll nurse me."

Two days before the holiday Berler solved our problem. He invited his staff to spend Christmas Eve at villa Vera. Surprisingly, out of twenty-five, thirteen of us accepted. It gave me cause to look at those other eleven, wondering whether they had the same problem as Maria and I. Berler's invitation also left me wondering. It could, of course, have been merely a last minute decision to liven up the holiday for his young motherless son. But I felt there was something more to it.

I went to Konstancin ahead of time to help the governess at Berler's home decorate the tree with cardboard angels and cotton snow and it was I who climbed the ladder to fasten the silver Christmas star to the topmost branch.

The table was set for sixteen people of which thirteen might be imposters like myself and Maria.

Was it possible that Berler knew?

Berler was a puzzle to me. Officially he was a German. He owned a large, prosperous business, yet he frequently borrowed money. I remembered now that he would not have to repay the money he had borrowed from Kovalski, and oddly enough the same thing was true in regard to the money Fischer had prepaid for an order. Then I recalled that he still hadn't paid me for the night his customers had stayed in my room at the boarding house. Fortunately for me, I thought, not withstanding a certain anxiety, the amount he owed me was not very large.

I was also puzzled by certain ambiguities in his private life. There seemed to be no woman in his life at present. But there were women who occasionally appeared for a day or two. These, he treated liberally. Two of them he had introduced as former wives. A *Frau* Schuster supposedly was his sister, a younger woman, his daughter, and ever so often some female would enter his office without knocking as if she were a close friend, but I never saw any of them again.

During the first inventory at the metal plant a Torah was found. When we asked Berler what to do with it, he took it as a souvenir for his son. But the day of the Christmas party, when I had followed the governess to the attic to get the Christmas decorations, I'd caught a glimpse of the Torah wrapped in a white cloth in the same trunk as the decorations.

A Torah in the attic; a Christmas tree in his living room. Was Berler sitting at the head of the table consciously playing host to thirteen homeless Jews?

All sixteen voices were uplifted — despite suspicion, despite dread — in the lovely strains of "Silent Night, Holy Night . . ."

22

Jan Kulok, the engineer who had brought Frania to Warsaw, often came to the capital to buy plumbing parts for the German company who employed him in Rava-Ruska. Each time he brought money and letters for Frania and conveyed messages to her from our oldest sister Anna. He had been a steady customer in Anna's fabric store and when she asked him to take Frania under his wing on one of his trips to Warsaw, she introduced her as a young Christian friend who had never travelled before, feeling sure that such company would automatically place Frania beyond the suspicion of the fellow-passengers.

In all good faith this engineer had done the most natural thing upon their arrival in Warsaw when Frania could not reach me and checked her into a hotel. Only later did he discover that Anna and Frania were sisters, and as yet he did not know of my relationship to them.

Jan looked much younger than his actual forty and was not unattractive despite his slight limp and a face too small for his huge body. His manner was kind, especially to Frania. He had taken a fancy to her and she seemed to reciprocate his feeling.

Frania had told me they were coming to visit. I left the gate open, and when I saw them walk up the drive, I went down to invite them in. But Jan, for reasons I would understand later, would not stay. Supporting himself on his rubber-tipped cane, he limped away. Frania looked at me. Her eyelids were red and swollen.

"Roma . . . I have terrible news."
"Don't call me Roma."
She burst into tears. "Who cares?"
I caught my breath. "What happened?"
"Jan saw Hersh —"
"And? Something has happened to Anna!"
She sobbed harder, grabbed my arm, and said, "Come upstairs."

Both Hersh and my brother Abner had been kept by the Germans at the Rava-Ruska Burying Camp. They were digging pits and burying a new cartload of corpses when a pale arm sticking out the heap seemed to point at Hersh. He was shocked to see a familiar stubby hand with short fingers. He moved closer and saw the engagement ring he had put on Anna's finger ten years before. Soon he found his mother, my sister Adela, and her husband, Abner's wife, Sara, and their baby Lisa.

Keeping an eye on the guard's booth near the main gate, Hersh and Abner began to dig an empty pit to separate their dead from the rest.

Suddenly, Abner became motionless . . . Hersh urged him to hurry before the guards noticed, but Abner was staring at little Lisa. He picked her up.

Hersh uttered warnings and pleaded with Abner. But Abner pressed his child to his heart, fondled her, whispering endearing names. All at once, he threw the dead child into the grave, shoved Hersh aside and, taking his shovel with him ran off. Hersh called after him to come back. But Abner screamed curses over his shoulder and kept running toward the exit. He held the shovel he had used to dig a grave for his family as a weapon, ready to hit anyone who got in his way.

The guard at the exit gate raised his gun and fired. Abner fell.

The guard called Hersh over and ordered him to take Abner away. "Throw the swine into the pit," he said.

Hersh tried to pick up his brother-in-law, but he wasn't strong enough. He was forced to drag him by an arm along the ground, hoping he could revive him when the guard looked the other way.

Many a sleepless night I had blamed myself for Father's deportation. Now I blamed myself for Abner's death. Both of them had been arrested by the Russian Occupational Forces in 1940 for the "crime" of being wealthy. At that time I had done all I could and succeeded in having them released. I was then hailed as a miracle worker and friends and enemies alike came to me for advice on how to help their own arrested relatives.

But had I not succeeded in freeing them, Father's fate would never have been to find himself in the Market Place of Niemirov amidst other Jews assembled for deportation. He would never have sat there on his suitcase chanting prayers, quietly accepting God's will. He would be praying somewhere else now — and Abner would be alive. Both of them would have been tried and would have received the usual sentence: Ten years in a Russian prison. A haven!

I wished I were dead.

Yet, I did everything to stay alive.

The next time Jan Kulok came to Warsaw he had more news for us. He had learned how Anna, Adela, little Lisa and Hersh's mother died. They had all been hidden in Anna's house, in the crawl-space between two floors constructed by Hersh which Frania had described to me in great detail. The *Sonderkommando* (Special Command) had finished searching the house and were on their way out, when Lisa began to cry. They ripped the false floor up and hauled the family out. Then they shot all of them in the backyard.

On several occasions Jan had requested Hersh "the plumber" for work outside the camp. Recently, when he had asked for him, he had been told by the camp office that the "plumber" was no longer there.

Jan was convinced that Hersh was neither dead nor deported, but that he had escaped and was hiding in the woods.

One evening when Jan had come home late he was told by his housekeeper that a strange looking man had been there to see him. The man, she said, was dressed like a peasant but didn't look like one. He had been very disappointed not to find Jan home, and had scribbled something on a matchbox and asked her to give it to him. The housekeeper, a cautious woman, had deemed it wise to hide this message and had put the matchbox first in one place and then in another and finally could not recall where she had hidden it. They searched and searched but could never find it.

"What did the message say?" I asked.

"You don't know my housekeeper. She would never read a message meant for my eyes only. At least, so she claims. But I am certain that that peasant was Hersh because her description fits him."

I damned the housekeeper for her discretion and hoped against hope that Hersh — whom I loved, who had conveyed to me my father's blessings, who had persuaded Frania to leave Rava-Ruska — was alive.

I told Berler I was sick and buried myself in villa June.

23

It was April 1943; Konstancin was in bloom.

Zosia brought me the news that the inmates of the Warsaw Ghetto had risen in armed resistance.

The things she told me sounded so incredible that I just listened and shook my head in disbelief.

The best source for real information was the Vaclava family so I had to come out of my self-imposed isolation. After three weeks of sick-leave I came back to work.

As I expected, Bronislav, an important officer in the Polish underground, had brought home the *Bulletyn Informacyjny,* an underground newspaper. It stated that a few hundred Germans in armored vehicles had entered the Ghetto with the intention of liquidating it. Bronislav confirmed what Zosia had said that the Jews, "as unbelievable as it may seem," had actually repelled the German troops.

In my room on Chmielna Street I heard the detonations; I heard machine guns rattling in the Ghetto.

Through lies and deception, I had hacked out an almost "normal" way of life for myself while my people rose to a dignity I would never reach.

Raging inside I asked Bronislav politely why the Polish underground didn't use this favorable moment to strike at the enemy.

"The decisions are made by the Exile Government. Perhaps

soon we will," he answered just as politely. Then he went on: "The
Jews are putting up a great fight. It's amazing. They're using
homemade Molotov Cocktails, waterpipes, captured German
weapons, anything. Who would believe it? We thought it would be
over in four days and now it's three weeks. We made an attempt to
get ammunition to them through the underground tunnel but the
Germans discovered it. They filled the tunnel with poison gas and
sealed it off. Three Poles got trapped there."

Three Poles and they had given up!

At the beginning of May the Germans set fire to the Ghetto
and it raged for six days. The battle still went on.

Red tongues of fire seemed to lick the pale sky. German
planes, like black birds of prey, dived dropping incendiary bombs.
Fire geysers spewed fountains of brilliant yellow and orange, and
clouds of thick smoke rolled up from the walled Jewish city, one
piling on top of the other like a gigantic grey mountain. The murk
spread and spread until it blanketed all of Warsaw.

It was the biggest fire in Europe.

A month after Zosia had brought me the news, shooting was
still going on. Then, one day Bronislav came to tell me the news.
Nearly fainting, I feigned indifference: "You mean it's all over?" I
asked in a neutral voice.

"It seems so," he said.

"What do you know about those inside?"

"People say that behind those walls it's 'Dante's Inferno,' but
that's not for the ears of a young girl like you."

"We're all in this together. I want to hear about it . . ."

"They're tossing their children out of the windows. They're
jumping from third and fourth floors. There's a sickening stench of
burned flesh. The streets are covered with their dead. But driven,
the Lord alone knows by what, half the dead go on fighting. At
night they disappear into a network of tunnels they've dug. In the
morning those mutilated, lacerated, bloody shadows are out again
fighting — I hope we measure up to them when the time comes."

This was the first time I had heard admiration for my people
from a Pole. Now it came, after so many had been killed.

"The time for *us* is now," I said. "What are we waiting for?"

"An order from our leaders in London."

"How can they judge the situation from there?"

Bronislav shrugged.

After fourty-eight days there were no more bomb detonations
to be heard. Only machine guns rattling now and then.

Only a very few Jews came out from the tunnels alive. And then some of them were denounced by Poles.

They all must have known from the beginning that they could never win, just as Abner must have known the futility of attacking an armed guard with a shovel in his hands.

24

Rolf was back.

His radiance was gone, he was thinner, paler, more remote. Outwardly he was as loving as he had been, but his thoughts seemed to be elsewhere.

During the first weekend we spent at villa June, I tried to find out what had hurt him. At first he spoke only in generalities. Witebsk had been a mess: orders contradicting each other; his unit under constant bombardment; Germans constantly being harassed by partisans, even in broad daylight; Germans going from one building to another, disappearing, never to be seen again. Morale had disintegrated completely.

Then, shuddering, he told me how local Russians were picked up at random and loaded into vans, but instead of being taken away the van driver would push a button that released poisoned gas. Afterwards the van was driven to an open ditch, the corpses had been dumped, and the vehicle would return for a fresh load.

Rolf, his shoulders slumped, stared at the floor.

Had he perhaps been forced to operate such a van?

He looked up and met my eyes. "I couldn't help them," he said. "Finally I managed to rescue a few Jews after I had myself been assigned to a Jew detecting squad. It was easy to declare some Jews to be Tatars when I learned Tatars were circumcised as well."

Why was he sitting like that if he had not driven such a van? Suddenly the pity died in my heart leaving only a burning need to know the truth. "Why didn't you ask to be assigned to drive such a van?"

He looked at me with puzzlement and horror.

"You could have let the victims escape," I said.

His head fell forward once more. "They didn't need drivers," he said in a low voice. "They had plenty of drivers."

I took him in my arms and kissed his poor drawn face. How could he know that the help he had given my friends could never be enough for me, that my heart was insatiable. I did not realize then that my distrust of him was the result of my own guilt feelings; to love a German meant betrayal of my people.

Even later when I learned that Rolf had been an active member of the Polish resistance movement, there were comparatively few moments of incredible happiness, and then this news became just another item on the credit sheet I felt it necessary to keep on his behalf. He had refrained from burdening me sooner than he had to with that information.

Only when Bronislav had to leave home and go into hiding did Rolf call upon me to become the contact between them. Despite his reluctance to have me actively involved, I became the courier who would take to Bronislav the permits that he forged and the revolvers that he stole.

Bronislav risked coming home one night to tell me that two important members of his organization had been arrested by the Criminal Police. "They were caught with guns in their possession and will be shot," he said. "I want Rolf to know about it before the case is referred to the Gestapo. Perhaps he can work a miracle . . ."

"The two guns found on the youths are material evidence," Rolf said when I told him the story. "But it is conceivable that both guns were owned by one of them. The other could claim that when he saw the police coming he was afraid to return the gun openly to his friend to whom it belonged. Everybody knows boys are curious about firearms. There's a good possibility that he could be let off with a reprimand for keeping bad company. We should try. Perhaps one can be saved."

Bronislav took the message to his superior and both nearly went out of their minds making the choice between Zdislav and Staszek. Rolf instructed Staszek what to say and he was released within a few days. Zdislav was delivered to the Gestapo.

My liaison-work between Rolf and Bronislav kept me informed on matters I would never normally hear about. I carried information to Bronislav that Berlin had a special mission in Warsaw to ferret out the channels the underground used to transmit messages to the Polish Exile Government. It so happened that the mission was quartered in Rolf's apartment building.

One evening Rolf called and invited me to breakfast at Switez Coffeehouse on Marszalkovska Street. Decoded, this conversaton meant that a raid had been scheduled at that hour on that particular block. Some other time, he called me and invited me for lunch at the Polanka Coffeehouse, or he asked me to meet him near the main post office. I promptly forwarded the information through Vaclava to Bronislav who dispatched a message from underground headquarters that suspects should stay clear of this particular block. Other messages I carried from Rolf directly to Bronislav. They bore the German police seal and permitted the name bearer to walk the streets after curfew. Often Rolf picked me up at the office after work and dropped a heavy paper package I was to deliver to Bronislav, into my large pigskin pocketbook.

One afternoon Rolf came to pick me up at work. He had no package for me that day. We walked home to Chmielna Street. He seemed sad and depressed. I handed him his accordion after we arrived. It never failed to work its magic in lifting his spirits.

"Not today, Cecylia . . ."

"Have you been assigned to Russia again?"

"It's nothing like that." He sat down at the table, put his elbows on it, and took his head in his hands. "Sit down, near me. Let me hold your hand."

I did as he asked.

"Yesterday I was assigned to supervise two Polish officers. We raided the aprtment of an extortionist on Aleje Jerozolimskie and arrested him. Cowering in a corner behind a cupboard we found a man who had no identification papers. In the presence of the two Polish policemen, I had no other choice but to take him along. As I suspected, he was a Jew. He admitted it later in my office. He said he was an attorney, recently escaped from the Ghetto, and gave his name as Kahane. He answered all my questions without resistance as if resigned to his fate.

"I handed him a printed form assuming that a lawyer would know what it was. 'Why are you showing me a discharge certificate?' he asked. I took it back and told him to give me a Polish name so that I could fill out the form.

" '*Herr Kommissar,*' he said, awarding me an instant promotion by this form of address, 'Why do you torment me in the face of death? I have already admitted to being a Jew. What else do you want?' His voice was indifferent, his face expressionless. He had said that he was thirty-two, but he seemed closer to fifty and he looked at me as if to say I was welcome to what was left of him.

"I went and put my hand on his shoulder and told him I meant to release him but I couldn't do it under the name of Kahane. 'I told you I was a Jew,' he said.

" 'I know,' I said, 'That's why it is imperative that you be discharged today. Tomorrow I may not be able to do it.'

"He fell to his knees and clasped my legs and began to sob — I felt dirty . . . Like never before."

It had become clear a long time ago that Rolf had crossed over to the other side.

One night, our arms wrapped around each other, he told me the snapshot fragment of Bruno's face haunted him in his dreams. Despite my repeated description of every feature, he said he was unable to fill in the missing part of the photograph. "Hitler is not only destroying the Jews and other people he calls subhuman, he is killing the souls of his own people."

Julek's friend was arrested on the charge of murder. To be accused of murder or any other ordinary crime, was preferable to the accusation of being Jewish.

Criminals were tried and sentenced, according to criminal law. However, in this case, when Rolf looked into the man's file he found in addition the word JEW stamped in large red letters across the first page.

He learned of an order given by Banisch, the Chief of Police: Criminals detained in jail for more than two months awaiting trial were to be released.

Rolf removed the first page and antidated the man's arrest so that he fell into the category of those to be released.

Another time Julek asked for help for himself.

One day he phoned urging me in his usual undertone to meet him at a restaurant across the street from his house. I went during my lunch hour.

There he told me that he had asked his wife, Teresa, to buy a razor for him and to meet him afterwards at a certain street corner. He had waited for half an hour and then had gone home. Just as he was turning into his street, Teresa's thirteen-year-old sister, Ursula, intercepted him and warned him to stay away because

Teresa had been picked up on the street by a Polish plainclothesman who had escorted her home. While the policeman was questioning the landlady, Ursula had managed to get out.

She was advised to hide out in the living quarters of my friend, Edmund Diller, the physician from Przemysl, and Julek was to spend the night at his sister's place.

25

I called Rolf.

While we were waiting for him, we saw Teresa being led from the house to a car and driven away. By the time Rolf arrived Julek had bitten his lips bloody. Rolf listened to Julek's story and said he would see what he could do.

That evening I learned that Rolf had gone to see Teresa in jail and had instructed her not to admit anything. Then he had faked a showdown with the Polish plainclothesmen, pretending outrage over the fact that this poor Catholic girl had been exposed to such a traumatic experience. The Polish official, frightened by the German, immediately filled out papers for Teresa's release which were to be signed by his superior in the morning.

I phoned Julek at his sister's home and told him the good news. He asked me to meet him at the Caffee Polanka near my office the next day after work.

I arrived first and to celebrate Rolf's accomplishment, I ordered an éclair. Where in the world was Julek? I waited another fifteen minutes and left.

At Vaclava's I found Rolf waiting for me. Julek had not come because now he was in jail too.

He had sent Ursula to their apartment to pick up some money even though Rolf had warned him that the place might be watched.

On her way out the police had grabbed her, and slapped her till she had taken them to Julek, who spent the night at his sister's. His sister and her husband were also arrested.

They all admitted being Jewish and were promptly taken to the Paviak Prison.

"Now, I'm in real trouble," Rolf said. "That Polish policeman came to my office. You should have heard how sarcastic he sounded. — 'Too bad, Mr. Rechter. They've admitted they're Jews. Better luck next time . . .' "

"Now he's got a hold over you!" I said.

"He won't denounce me since he can't gain anything by it. But he'll ask for favors."

We assumed that Julek and his family had been shot in the Paviak prison yard as were most Jews who were found hiding behind false identities. However, three months later Julek appeared at Frania's, on Creditova Street.

When he was arrested Julek's money had been taken from him. He was separated from his family and since he had said that he was an electrician, he had been set to work instead of being shot.

Sometime later he was assigned to the open truck that daily went to fetch bread from an outside bakery. For weeks he planned to escape in this fashion and on that particular morning he managed to do it.

His return rekindled the hope that some day my father, Perele, Mark, Fischer, and all those who had disappeared, would return as well.

Julek had lost fifteen kilo. His nose had grown longer and his ears larger. He cried a lot. Perhaps he felt guilty because he had sent for his money, thus bringing about the death of so many he loved.

I told him I was willing to buy him new counterfeit papers and to pay for his living expenses and he stopped crying for a time, only to start again when he began to list the difficulties he would have in obtaining those papers and in finding a place to stay.

Meanwhile, without documents he had to be confined to Frania's room.

Whatever he had once done for her it was nothing compared to what Frania now did for him. She shopped for food and prepared it; she carried his chamberpots to the communal bathroom located at the end of the hallway so that he would not be seen by the landlady and her two teenage sons. She never complained and even volunteered to contribute toward his expenses.

In order to get the photograph needed for a forged *Kennkarte* Julek had to walk to a photographer's studio and without a *Kenn-*

karte it was dangerous to take such a risk. It was a vicious circle. In any case, how long could his presence at Frania's be kept a secret?

Again Rolf came to our rescue.

He told me that Bronislav, believing that a Polish insurrection was imminent and wanting to reciprocate for the services Rolf had rendered to Poland, had given him an "Iron Letter" from the Polish underground. It stated what Rolf had done for the cause and called upon all Poles to assist him during the coming upheaval and give him protection if he had to go into hiding until the expected slaughter of Germans was over.

Bronislav urged Rolf to learn a little Polish, at least enough so that he could say a few words to hold off the first Pole who might want to strike him before seeing the document. He had also given him a *Kennkarte* bearing Rolf's photograph and a Polish name.

"We don't look alike," Rolf said, "But for whatever it's worth, I'm going to lend the *Kennkarte* to Julek."

"But what will happen to you in case of an emergency?" I asked.

"*This is* an emergency. I'll tell Bronislav that I lost mine and he'll get me another."

"The emergency might come sudden and soon," I said.

"I'll be all right. Didn't I keep my promise to come back from Russia?"

"Why didn't you show me the "Iron Letter" sooner?"

"I wanted you to be involved as little as possible."

"But if they found it on you?"

"Don't worry, they'll never find it."

Julek, in Rolf's civilian suit, equipped with Rolf's false *Kennkarte*, went to his appointment with a Polish friend. This friend had located a Polish woman dedicated to the aid of politically persecuted Poles and Julek, a former inmate of the Paviak Prison, fitted her requirements. She took him into her apartment in Praga, a suburb of Warsaw.

Julek came to me at Vaclava's once a month to collect money for his rent and other expenses. But when he started to come more often, I became nervous. He complained he was bored, spending all his time in a room alone, and welcomed any excuse to talk to someone. I warned him that it was dangerous but it didn't help.

And one day, only six months after he had escaped from the Paviak Prison, he went for a walk and never came back to his quarters.

26

One calamity followed another.

The underground reported Bronislav missing. Apparently, in a case in which Rolf could be of no help, he had made contact with another German by the name of Klang who had promised to get an underground comrade out of the Paviak Prison. Ignoring Rolf's advice to stay away from Klang, who was suspect, Bronislav had gone to meet him. The underground, convinced that Bronislav was in the hands of the Gestapo, alerted Rolf to be careful.

"Do you think he'll talk?" I asked Rolf.

"A man's breaking point can't be guessed," Rolf answered.

"Then you must hide somewhere."

Rolf got his uniform cap, reached inside the sweat band, and drew forth a strip of folded paper. It was the "Iron Letter."

I read and reread it, and felt closer to Rolf than ever before. I embraced him and said: "I think it would be wise to make use of it now."

Holding me in his arms he said: "If I disappeared *now, you'd* have the Germans on your neck. I can't let that happen."

"Then I'll have to disappear as well. The underground will help me too."

"We'll keep our eyes and ears open," Rolf said.

"Stay with me tonight, I'm frightened."

We were still asleep in the morning when Vaclava knocked at the door. "Someone to see you," she said.

It took me a while to collect myself. I yawned and complained: "What next? Now they come early in the morning. There is no end to this misery."

It was Maria.

She looked so ghastly that Rolf, without a word, poured her a glass of vodka, waited for her to swallow it, and led her to a chair.

Maria, who was always the first to get to the office in the morning, had found Berler, on the floor dead; strangled. Tables, chairs, and desks were overturned, papers strewn around. A young shipping clerk lay dead in another office, and next to him, the governess of Berler's little boy. They, too, had been strangled. Maria had run straight to me.

"Don't go to work today," Rolf said to both of us. "Stay here until you hear from me."

My suspicion that thirteen of Berler's employees were imposters like myself was now strongly fortified, for they stayed home, waiting too.

It was Vaclava who related the rumors that had been circulating in the Vinetta offices: Berler was a spy; Berler was a double agent; he had been killed over a woman; a jealous woman had hired a killer; Berler was a Jew.

Rolf, however, puzzled by the strange way in which this triple murder was being handled by the police, suspected that the Gestapo had simply disposed of a suspect German. The killing of the other two had been an unforeseen necessity.

A colonel, whom Berler had claimed to be his brother and of whom he had spoken frequently, did not make an appearance at his funeral. Of his other relatives only *Frau* Schuster was present. It seemed to confirm our earlier doubts as to whether the other women who had come to see him were actually his daughters or his wives.

Berler remained a mystery to us in death as in life. The murder was not investigated and the rumors died away. Some of the thirteen who had been guests at Berler's Christmas dinner came back to work, others left. Vinetta went under new management.

27

I was looking for a new job.

One day, after a number of interviews, I felt more tired than usual. On the way to Vaclava's my longing for Bruno suddenly became so intense that I went to Belveder Station to get the train to Konstancin. Only behind the locked doors of the desolated villa June did I feel free enough to totally immerse myself in fantasies about my child.

By the time I arrived it was six o'clock. I walked quickly through the snow-covered Main Street. But in the deeper snow of the lonely path through the woods I was forced to go more slowly. In places the snow drifts were knee high.

It was difficult to open the gate of villa June. My feet and my hands felt frozen. Only the thought of the electric heater in my room and my sense of nearness to Bruno gave me enough strength to make it through the driveway and up the stairs.

The electricity was not functioning.

I had to feel my way up to my room and into a drawer where there was a remedy for such an eventuality. I lit a match, and then a candle. Then I lit the primus stove and made some tea. Lastly I took the remnant of Bruno's photograph from its hiding place in the lining of my pocketbook.

It only took a few moments to bring him to life.

For an hour we were really together.

I bathed him, watched him hit the surface of the bath-water

118

with his palms and wondered why he was so thin that I could count his ribs. Then I had him wrapped in a towel in my arms and, feeling the warmth of his slender body, buried my face in his soft hair and kissed the mole on his left shoulder. I rubbed noses with him, talked baby-talk, and finally tucked him into his bed and hummed a lullaby until he fell asleep.

After a time I remembered Rolf.

What would he think when he came to Vaclava's and she wouldn't be able to tell him where I had gone?

I looked through the window but the crystal flowers coating the panes obscured my view. It was dark already and it was impossible to see whether it had begun to snow again. I could still catch the last train, but I knew I wouldn't leave, not yet. Besides, I had promised Bruno I would stay close to him that night.

In the morning, cold, unwashed, hungry, I arrived in Warsaw. At the Belveder Station a worried Rolf was waiting for me. The night before, when he had gone to Vaclava's and I wasn't there he had assumed that I had gone to Konstancin. Vaclava had asked him for a particular document which he had managed to procure without authorization that morning. It was for a Pole who hopefully would become one of the leaders in future liberated Poland. He gave me the document to deliver to Vaclava, who had become the new go-between since Bronislav's disappearance. We then parted.

In the tramway to Chmielna Street, I noticed a sudden restlessness among the pasengers. Some German officers had boarded the car at the last stop and were checking papers as well as pocketbooks and parcels.

Rolf had taught me to sit near a tramway exit whenever I was undertaking a mission so that there would be at least a few minutes leeway before the investigators reached me. Meanwhile the tramway might reach a stop and I might be able to get off without attracting attention.

I stood up pretending to be straining to read the street signs as they flashed by and, luckily, the tramway slowed down. I was at the door and on the street before the tramway stopped, and, slipping on an icy step, fell into the slushy snow unable to move any further. My large brown pigskin pocketbook containing in its lining the remnant of Bruno's photograph and the unauthorized document had landed a few feet away, out of my reach.

The German officers jumped from the tramway and came towards me. Sympathetically, a crowd began to gather immediately and the Germans held them back, shouting that the injured woman needed air.

I looked in the opposite direction from where my handbag lay and prayed that some thief would steal it and run. Out of the corner of my eye I saw one of the Germans bend toward it and my heart seemed to stop. But he stood up and came over and handed me my property. If he saw me grow pale he must have thought it was from pain and in fact a few moments afterward I did lose consciousness.

When I came to later in the hospital I found out that I had broken a leg.

"How long have I been asleep?" I asked. The answer seemed to come from miles away: "We picked you up unconscious from the police building." It was the voice of a stranger. A woman's head in a nurse's cap bent over and straightened up the pillows under me.

When I felt myself again drifting off, I collected all my strength, and then I remembered:

Since the occupying Russian forces were interminably hammering home to us the slogan "Who doesn't work doesn't eat" over loudspeakers, I took a job selling musical instruments and sporting goods in a nationalized department store. Our family unit of three had been reunited in Lvov for a few months. Mark worked in a hotel as a bookkeeper. Although he looked down on his job as beneath him, he nust have been doing it well because his Russian boss had already promoted him twice.

Then, Father got the information from a local Communist that he and six other "rich" men living in Niemirov were to be deported to Siberia. He fled in the dark of the night and came to me. Perele and Blume followed.

Through my connections in the department store, he and his family were permitted to register with the Lvov police, a privilege usually closed to newcomers to the city. I was also able to get a job in a bank for Blume.

Our way of life had changed for the worse, but our conviction that the change was a temporary one made it almost bearable.

Until Father and Blume were arrested.

He who went three times daily to the synagogue and devoted the rest of his time to studying the Torah, was accused of being an active blackmarketeer. Blume also was taken along.

I took sick-leave so as to use all my influence to help. I in-

tervened in many places and after three days Blume was released from jail. Luckily her boss, the Russian bank director didn't mind claiming that Blume was indispensable.

After interrogating me, the investigator, a Russian Captain, promised he would let Father go also, but not before his wife appeared before him to answer a few questions.

Perele, her velvety almond-shaped eyes fixed on me, said in a soft voice: "You are a courageous girl, Roma —" She handed me our family jewelry, took a nightbag, and went with me to the police.

I waited in the corridor.

After ten minutes she came out with red blotches on her face and told me that she never had expected to see me again.

The same Captain then asked me to bring my brother Abner for questioning. He would only let my father go after that. I brought a reluctant Abner to the police and stood waiting in the corridor during the interrogation. After half an hour a policeman came out of the Captain's office and ordered me to go home.

Abner had been detained.

Realizing that my wish to help my father had only drawn my brother into the trap, I suddenly felt ill and fainted.

In the morning, the doctor told me that, although my condition was not serious, he would have to keep me in the hospital for another three days to make some tests.

Everyone except Abner and my father who were still detained rallied around my bedside. Blume, Perele, my new friend Fischer and my landlord Brustiger-Kovalski came to see me every day. Mark's absence was obvious and embarrassing. Everyone tried to brush aside my questions concerning him.

Not until I got home, did I find that Mark had panicked and taken and left for Zloczov.

28

At the hospital they told me my temperature was high. After taking some X-rays the doctor said they would have to operate to set the leg, and it would be immobilized in a cast for several weeks.

The next morning I swallowed some pills, I groaned, had a mask put over my face and then . . .

. . . I was lying in a place I had never seen before. Not knowing where I was, I pulled the sheet over my face burying myself in fear like a child. Through the sheet I saw shadows enter the room. My sisters Anna and Adela came gliding towards me noiselessly. They were performing some kind of dance. Anna, the oldest, grabbed my sick leg and pulled me along with them laughing. Round and round they dragged me. The pain was unbearable. "Come with us," Anna said and her blue eyes glittered.

I wanted to say that I could not go because of my broken leg. But my lips were sealed by something. Slowly, I realized what it was. What dried my mouth was a chemical the Germans used to prevent the Poles from singing their national anthem before execution.

I stared at Anna dumbly.

She took my arm and dragged me out of the room. "She's shamming, she's always shamming," she cried.

Outside Abner held up a shovel and shouted: "Traitor!"

My whole body contracted in expectation of the coming blow, but just then little Lisa cried, "Daddy, Daddy, the ship has come here."

Drowsy and nauseated I awoke for a moment, only to fall again into a sickly, haunted sleep.

Rolf was bending over my bed, wiping perspiration from my forehead. He asked me what I had been dreaming.

"I don't remember . . ." I said. Then I added: "Maybe that I was crippled for life —"

He bent down and kissed my lips. "No matter what happens — we'll be together."

I wanted to burst out with the words, 'I love you,' which he longed to hear, but instead I closed my eyes again.

My recovery was slow. But when I realized that I was safe in the hospital, that apparently the Germans never came on raids there, I considered it a haven, a sunlit clearing in the darkness of the jungle outside.

The white uniformed nurses passing by my open door seemed like angels to me. The antiseptic odors coming from the corridors were drowned by the scent of Rolf's roses on my night table. I wondered where he had got them at that time of the year. Even the night cries of patients in pain did not depress me.

The false hope that I could remain in the cocoon until the end of the war was, of course, disappointed when the cast was taken off and I was released once again to make my way in a hostile dangerous world. Rolf took me in a rickshaw to Vaclava's and there carried me up four flights of stair.s

Henceforth I would limp and have to walk with the help of a cane.

29

I was working again.

My new boss, the owner of a battery factory, was Polish.

Although Poles were more apt to smell out Jewish origins beneath a false facade, I had to take that risk, for being without an *Arbeitskarte* (work card) was the greater threat. Caught in a raid without an *Arbeitskarte* I would be deported to Germany to work in an ammunition factory where fellow-Poles who shared the same fate would easily detect my secret.

One morning Rolf surprised me in my new office.

"Don't let the boss see you," I said.

I led him to the waiting room and he told me he had bought a motorcycle and was learning how to drive it.

"Is it hard?" I asked.

"It's almost like riding a bicycle. It's terrific fun." He paused. "Listen, darling, will you do me a favor and drop my watch off to be cleaned? It's on your way home and I can't spare the time now."

Was that why he had come by?

"Take it to a reputable jeweler," he went on. "It's an expensive watch; it's got a gold case."

"Will I see you tonight?"

"I'll know later. Can you step out for a second?" he said.

Wondering, I followed him to the hallway.

"Do you love me?"

He accepted my silence, used to it by now.

"You still cannot say it. Some day you will. Kiss me."

I took his face in my hands and kissed his right eye and his left eye.

He pressed me to him tightly. But I heard a door open and pulled away and hurried to my desk.

In the afternoon when I called Schleger answered the phone. He said that Rolf had not as yet come back from the hearing at Aleja Szucha.

"From where?" I gasped.

"Well, from the Gestapo."

The Gestapo! "Oh, you mean . . ." I pretended to know.

"Yes, the hearing for which he was supoenaed."

". . . What time was he supposed to be back?"

"One never knows with such things."

Dazed, I hung up.

He had given me the watch as a farewell gift!

I called Schleger a few times, but it was always, "No, he has not returned yet."

As the afternoon wore on Rolf's colleagues and his superior grew concerned. Apparently not even *Kommissar* Korben dared to call the Gestapo to inquire about his lieutenant.

After the office closed at five, I ran to Frania. She tried to comfort me as well as she could, but then she shocked me by saying: "When this blows over why don't you two get married?"

"He's a German."

"So what, you love each other."

"I could never do that to our father."

"Don't you remind me a hundred times what Father used to say: 'A man who saves one human life saves the whole world.' It's something from the bible. Rolf has saved so many lives that Father would more than give his blessing."

I stared at her.

"Sssh!" said Frania. "Do you hear what I do? That's Rolf whistling." She ran to the door and I to the window.

A few minutes later I was in Rolf's arms.

"Finally, I've found you," he cried. "I went to your office but it was closed. I went to Vaclava's to look for you . . ."

He told me the Gestapo had called to ask how much he knew about Bronislav Gorski, how he happened to be fooled by Teresa and Julek, and whether the name Kovalski meant anything to him. Rolf replied that he had been introduced to all four by Berler.

The subsequent questions had been put to him in a polite, almost in a friendly tone. He had expected my name to come up and was vastly relieved that it had not.

"Are you sure everything is alright?"

He nodded. "It's now written in my Gestapo file that I am fanatically devoted to the cause. Therefore, Cecylia darling, may I have my watch back?"

Our sense of security was shaken two weeks later.

Rolf confided to me rather reluctantly that the Gestapo had called him again. They had informed him that his interpreter, Schleger, the *Volksdeutscher*, was a traitor and that there were reasons why he had to be eliminated discreetly. So Rolf was being given the honor of finishing him off. On the pretext of his having to interrogate a political prisoner in the Paviak Prison, he was to take along his interpreter and shoot him in a passageway.

Rolf reported back to the Gestapo with the information that there was too much traffic in the Paviak corridors and that twice he had missed good opportunities to take Schleger by surprise.

He knew his excuse would give him only a temporary reprieve, but he hoped somehow to find a way out of his dilemma.

The next morning when he arrived at his office he was introduced to a new interpreter and was told that his colleague had been sent to Russia.

"It's time for you to hide," I pleaded with Rolf.

"Soon, very soon, my darling."

The Gestapo then left Rolf alone and we relaxed.

30

In the beginning of June 1944, the interpreter newly assigned to Rolf gave him two tickets to a play which he said, Fraulein Szarek would especially enjoy. I usually refused to go to the theater, dances or parties when I could think of legitimate reasons, but the rumor of a planned plot against Hitler's life put me in such a good mood that I consented to top our private celebration with an evening out.

Later, on July 20, 1944, the attempt to assassinate Hitler took place. Twenty-three Germans had gathered around his table when a planted bomb off, but failed to kill Hitler.

As we left the theater, we heard the sound of nearby shooting. Instinctively we hit the pavement and were left with the impression that the bullets missed by inches. It was too dark to see what had happened so we dismissed the incident from our minds since such things were commonplace at that time in Warsaw.

At Chielna Street we rang the bell and waited for the janitor to unlock the entrance door. Rolf insisted upon bringing me to my room, betraying his concern for me.

After he left, I ran to the window and waited to catch another glimpse of him as he came out of the dark into the light of the corner streetlamp. He walked off to the right, his shadow growing longer and then disappearing. I could still hear him whistling a last "good night" as he normally did.

"It's so dark out there," I said to Vaclava who had joined me at the open window.

"Don't worry," she said softly. "He's well known in this neighborhood as our friend."

The following day, Rolf was half an hour late for our date at Vaclava's. When he finally arrived, I was unaccountably relieved and hugged him tight for a long time. He did not respond as he usually did by picking me up and whirling me around, and he ate little of the food I had served. I noticed for the first time that his uniform looked too large for him. I had the feeling that he was carrying a secret burden that he didn't want to share with me. Was it the imminent Polish uprising?

After I had removed the dishes, I said: "It's unwise for you to leave here so late at night."

He laughed and lit a cigarette. "You worried about me? You can't be serious. I'm worried aout you and that's what I want to talk about. Why don't you become *volksdeutsch?* For the duration of the war, I mean . . ."

So that's what it was. He was wracked with anxiety about me. If I became *volksdeutsch* I would be permitted to live in the German sector. Recently it had been fenced off from the rest of the city because, though a few of the dates predicted for a Polish uprising had passed without incident, the Germans had grown nervous. They had even issued orders to their men not to leave the sector after dark. At first Rolf had followed the orders but he had soon disobeyed them and come to see me.

He always shrugged off my plea that he stop being so foolhardy.

It was not the first time that Rolf had suggested I become *volksdeutsch.* Frania and my friends had urged me to do it, too. But I refused. Neither Frania nor Rolf knew of the irrational guilt I felt for not having remained with my family, and I did not intend to tell them about it now.

"*Kommissar* Korben promised to skip all the red tape and speed up your application," Rolf was saying. "You could move to my sector within the week. And it would make things so much easier for me. I could reach you without having to ask for a permit or breaking the law. And I could make sure that you are alright. I want you to live, darling." He smiled. "If there were an office for these matters, I would apply for an exchange: My life for yours."

I stared at him, too moved even to speak. Then I looked away. "It would be betrayal of everything my father stood for," I said softly.

"You loved your father that much?" Rolf asked.

All at once I had a momentary vision of my father as if I were present at the Market Place in Niemirov when he urged Abner to rescue his wife and leave him to his fate.

"I rejected his God," I said, "but I will love and respect his noble spirit all my life. I can't betray that."

Rolf took me in his arms.

". . . I feel so closely united with you — You don't know. For weeks, for months, a novel I read years ago has been haunting me. It is the story of a man who loved a blind woman, and to understand what life was like for her he blindfolded himself for two weeks. At the end of that time he believed he had finally penetrated the darkness of his beloved. But I doubt whether this could ever be true. After all, the man knew that at any moment the blindfold could be removed, and his sight restored." He paused as if he wanted to allow time for this to sink in, then he said: "I want to try to do the same thing, Cecylia. After the war, I want to become a Jew."

The following afternoon when the telephone rang at three o'clock, I was so sure it was Rolf's usual call that I said, "Yes, Rolf, this is Cecylia."

"*Fraulein* Szarek?" a male voice said. "This is *Herr* Schmidt."

He was a secretary to Banisch, the chief of the Criminal Police in Warsaw. I had met him once and Rolf had occasionally mentioned his name, saying that he was not as brutal as the others.

"Would you please come to my office?" Schmidt said.

"When do you want me to come?"

"Immediately, if possible."

My head was reeling. I recalled that at the time Fischer was under investigation he had been dismissed with praise only to be arrested a few weeks later. Perhaps the Gestapo had dismissed Rolf to arrest him now?

Schmidt led me through dreary empty corridors. The tapping of my cane on the cement floor of the corridor gave a hollow echo. I suddenly remembered that a forged document Rolf had asked me to deliver was still in my pocketbook.

The room I was taken to was not an office. It seemed to be a reception room and was rather pleasantly furnished with flowered upholstered chairs and matching draperies. It surprised me that the police building had a room like this.

Schmidt asked me to sit down. He reached for my hand and in a strangely sympathetic voice he said: "It is my duty to inform you that *Herr* Rechter was shot at 11:45 this morning."

"What do you mean?"

"He was shot through the heart."

"Where is he?" I was on my feet, staring wildly.

Schmidt put his hands on my shoulders and forced me gently back into my seat. "He has been shot through the heart," he repeated. "He died a martyr."

"I want to see him."

"You cannot."

"You must tell me where he is!"

"*Herr* Rechter is dead. At present he is in the morgue. He will be laid out at Aleja Szucha tomorrow. We'll inform you of the exact time of the funeral services."

Morgue. Funeral. They're lying to separate us forever.

"I want to see him."

Schmidt patted my hand. "*Fraulein* Szarek, please spare yourself the sight. Remember him as he was."

"I want to see him!"

"You need a permit for that."

"Who killed him?"

"The Polish underground."

"Where?"

"At Three Crosses Square."

"When?"

"I told you — 11:45 this morning."

Three Crosses Square? Where German police patrolled constantly and Polish police directed traffic? They really thought I was stupid. "Were the murderers captured?"

"It was a one-man job. He got away."

From Three Crosses Square? He couldn't really believe I would swallow that. "Tell me exactly how it happened."

He stepped back and began, in a patient, mechanical voice: "At 10 o'clock this morning the Chief ordered *Herr* Rechter to interrogate a prisoner held at the Paviak Prison. He was accompanied by his interpreter and a Polish plainclothesman. At the Three Crosses Square, in front of a camera store, the car stalled. The driver opened the hood and took out his tool kit. The interpreter suggested to *Herr* Rechter that they use the time to see

The author with Rolf Peschel in Warsaw (1942)

Rolf Peschel in his office (1942)

Plaque in the Alley of the Heroes at Yad Vashem in honor of Rolf Peschel.

הכנסת
KNESSET

Jerusalem, Feb. 5, 1987

Mrs.
Genia Rosenberg
Tel-Aviv.

Dear Mrs. Rosenberg,

Thank you ever so much for letting me have Sandra Brand's book "I dared to live." It is a remarkable book which I read almost spellbound, without putting it down. Mrs. Brand is blessed with an extraordinary gift of narration; her memory is amazing. The events which she had lived through are so different from the usual experiences of survivors and hence of special interest. When Mrs. Brand will be in Israel it will give me pleasure to meet with her.

Sincerely,

G. Gideon Hausner.

Letter from Gideon Hauser, general prosecutor at the trial of Adolf Eichmann. This letter led to the Hebrew translation of this book and helped begin the process of honoring Rolf Peschel as a Righteous Gentile.

what was available in the photo equipment store. *Herr* Rechter was just paying for a light meter when the driver sounded the horn to let them know that now they could proceed. As *Herr* Rechter and the interpreter left the store, a man stepped from the adjacent building and fired a machine gun. Both *Herr* Rechter and the interpreter fell dead. The Polish plainclothesman was wounded.

Now, I knew it was true. Rolf was dead.

Vaclava knew already. She was crying.

My eyes were dry and burning.

The underground was in turmoil. They had lost one of their most valuable members. They advised me to go into hiding and offered me any help I needed, for they knew that Rolf had been killed by his own people.

I listened but I did not hear. I would remain in Vaclava's apartment for the time being. Only one thing mattered. I had to see Rolf. I had to tell him something.

For two days *Kommissar* Korben was unavailable. I tried to see his assistant, Kruger — unavailable. I telephoned to Schmidt. He said that only the Chief of the police, Banisch, could get me a permit from the Gestapo, but Chief Banisch was unavailable. Time was running out.

That night I called Frania. Not even her uncontrollable weeping could break my cold, tearless calm.

In the morning a special messenger brought a printed announcement regarding the funeral service. It was now official. I was allowed to attend his funeral. The assembly point was the Police Headquarters at two P.M. the following day. Special tramways had been chartered to transport us to the cemetery. There was also a hand written note from Schmidt that I should be there two hours early.

"Why two hours early?" Frania asked over the phone. "Maybe they want to get rid of you before the funeral?"

Vaclava begged me not to go. When I said that I had to see Rolf before he was buried, she stared at me in silence.

At the specified time I met a smiling Schmidt at Police Headquarters. His boss had been successful in obtaining a permit for me to see Rolf in the chapel where he was laid out.

At Aleja Szucha, the headquarters of the Gestapo, I showed my written permit. I was sent from one offical in uniform to another, to a third and fourth, and then ushered into a large room dominated by a huge blown-up picture of Hitler.

Rolf's coffin was draped with the German flag and two additional flags on either side.

I limped to the bier, and laid both my hands on the blood-red flag. I said the words I had not been able to say when he was alive: "I love you, Rolf. I love you. Forgive me for not having told you so before."

31

Two Polish detectives escorted me to the last of three chartered tramways. The first two were reserved for Germans only. At the German section of the cemetery, the procession was formed according to rank and nationality. I was put behind the Germans of lowest rank.

A military band struck up a funeral dirge and we followed behind to the open grave. The eulogy was long and had nothing to do with the Rolf I knew. It was followed by roars of *Sieg. Heil! Sieg. Heil!* Salutes were fired and the coffin lowered.

I lingered while the crowd dispersed. Then I got down on my knees, put my cane beside the fresh grave, crossed myself and repeated: "I love you. Forgive me for not having told you so before."

I looked around at the countless identification tags in the German military cemetary and for some unaccountable reason I felt sorry for all those buried beneath.

When I rose and stared down the path to the main road, a tall woman fell in step beside me. "You took a great risk kneeling at the grave of a German," she said in Polish. "You're lucky these German officers let you get away with it. I saw them staring."

Her long face with its upturned nose seemed familiar.

"I had to pay him my last respects," I said.

She stopped, and we looked at one another.

"You don't recognize me, do you?" she said. "I was Mr. Rechter's cleaning woman."

I remembered. I nodded and we started to walk once more.

"I know something that should be of interest to you. That man you're so heartbroken about was not faithful to you," she said.

Now it was my turn to stop. I looked at her.

"You don't believe me?" She pointed with her finger to the right. "Mitzi Bringer is her name. She had an affair with him, and that I swear by Saint Antony. Why don't you look at her?"

"Leave me alone!" I heard my voice, thin and high like a child's.

"That German hussy works at the Criminal Police Headquarters and, take it from me, they had an affair."

I struggled, but my eyes, with a will of their own, opened wide and turned in the direction of the pointing finger. A beautiful young girl was looking at me, her face a mask of hate.

The tears that had not come before, suddenly brimmed in my eyes. I struggled to contain them but the next moment they were streaming down my cheeks.

The tall woman shook her head at me sympathetically.

Hiding my face with one hand I limped off.

At the exit my two Polish escorts were waiting for me. They had held up the third chartered tramway. The compassion the Polish detectives had seemed to have for me on the way to the cemetery was gone.

"Where have you been so long?" one of them reproached me. "We were due back half an hour ago. We'll be reprimanded because of you."

When we arrived at Police Headquarters we were told that some Poles had thrown grenades at the two tramways that left in time. A few passengers had been wounded and one had died on the way to the hospital.

No sooner had Vaclava heard the key turn in the lock, than she cried, "Jesus Christ! Am I happy to see you!"

Later she told me that the plan to avenge Rolf had been successfully carried out. She had followed orders from her organization not to warn me beforehand. I was, if possible, to be detained at home.

At first I was outraged at the idea that she was willing to have me sacrificed. But then I remembered how she had begged me not to attend the funeral.

Besides, Vaclava would not have hesitated to sacrifice herself for her cause.

32

I often wished, Rolf had been arrested and deported like Father and Perele, or like Fischer; then I could have kept on hoping for a reunion. But Rolf was dead. The one who had the right to live because of his German nationality was gone forever.

There were so many things I wanted to tell him.

Many times I picked up the receiver to ask the operator for his number and then I replaced it. Would I ever be able to accept this loss? Was life at all worth living?

Then thoughts about Mitzi Bringer haunted me. I had to see her.

At the sound of her voice over the phone I blushed from head to toe. Hesitantly, she consented to see me.

Frania cried over the phone that she would soon be mourning not only Rolf's death, but her sister's too. She said I was insane going to visit a German in the German district. "Remember how Bronislav never came back from that appointment with a German? And for what?"

She didn't know everything about Rolf. What he had done for Poles, what he had done for Jews. She didn't know that after this additional loss I now questioned whether it was worthwhile going on.

Neither she nor my friends dared to visit me at Vaclava's They were convinced that the house was under surveillance. According to them I was next on the list, and they thought it was a sort of suicide-attempt on my part to remain so visible, a ready target. A Jewish physician, Dr. Geisler from Lvov, also disguised as a Pole, came with his sister-in-law to try to take me away.

I didn't go. My room was permeated with Rolf's presence. I heard him whispering my name, his voice as real as it had been in the past. I smelled his scent in the dent of my pillow at night.

Let my enemy come for me. Frania was now finding her own way, and I was ready for the inevitable.

Mitzi Bringer's room was flooded with sunshine. It poured in through two large windows. The transparent curtains were drawn aside and gathered by silk cords. The rose-red drapes matched the tablecloth. Mitzi was dressed in red as well, apparently her favorite color. Her cheeks were rosy and her full mouth naturally pink. Seeing this healthy glowing girl at close range, I could understand what might have drawn Rolf to her.

She sat on the edge of a hard-backed chair and waited for me to speak. The silence had already lasted too long. Finally I said: "Please understand . . . I loved Rolf . . ."

"I know."

"I need your help."

"How can I be of any help?"

"I must know the truth," I said.

Mitzi bit her lip.

"Then it is true? Please," I begged with tears in my eyes.

"What is it you want?" she said coldly. "The juicy details? Do you want me to paint him black or white? And how about myself? Am I supposed to strip myself before you?"

It was really outrageous what I was asking of her. "Whatever you're telling me — I have to know."

She sat back in her chair. "I don't mean to be nasty. I happen to know how you feel." She played with the fringes on the tablecloth for a moment, and then she began: "When I was transferred from Germany here, shortly after my arrival, I was told that Rolf was seriously involved with a Polish girl and it was my job to make him interested in me. I told them I was engaged. But my boss insisted, said, the consequences for Rolf could be very bad and that it was my duty to lead him back to his own people. Well — I said, I'd try."

"I sought him out at our *Kameradschafts Abende* (Friendship Evening) and flirted a little. He wasn't too responsive. After a while it became more of a personal challenge than an assignment.

One night, while we were dancing together . . . I can't explain it, it happened all of a sudden, I wanted him badly." Her face flushed.

I stole a glance at her well-shaped legs and imagined her dancing with Rolf. I never had. Had he been open to her approaches because I was limping with a cane?"

"At one of our *Kameradschafts* Evenings, he played the piano. On our way home I asked him to play some more at his place. He agreed. Upstairs we kissed, but that was all. He was nice to me, but . . . perhaps it was the liquor . . . I don't know how to put it . . . You know what I mean? — Nothing came of it."

"And the next time?" I asked.

"There was no next time."

I left Mitzi Bringer's apartment in a strange mood. I had expected to find a little tramp, but instead I liked her.

I headed for a flower shop, bought eighteen red roses, and went to the cemetery.

In order to keep the German cemetery uniform, it was forbidden to place flowers on a grave. Therfore, I hid the roses under my coat as I passed through the gate. At the graveside I stuck the stems, one by one, into the soil, glancing repeatedly over my shoulder to make sure no one was in sight. Then I said loudly: "I love you, Rolf, I love you."

Limping toward the exit I was sure at twenty-seven my life was over.

I took the train to Konstancin, counting the minutes till I could break down and cry in Frania's arms.

"Oh, it's you," Frania greeted me. "I should have told you not to come. Jan is going to Cracow, and is taking me along. I've been cooped up here long enough. I'm just dying to see Cracow. You don't mind, do you?"

"No," I said.

33

O n my way back to Warsaw I thought of Rolf's mother. By the time I arrived at Belveder Station, I longed so desperately for contact with him that I went straight to the post-office and sent her a telegram. But after I had sent it off, I was frightened. How much did she know about me? Might she not disapprove of me and my relationship with her son? What would we say to each other?

A few days later she was at the door of Vaclava's apartment. She had come straight from the railroad station. Small and tense, she stood before me with her suitcase. She had Rolf's eyes set in a pale, worn face. My apprehension disappeared.

Over a glass of tea, I explained to her that she was entitled to a good hotel and to transportation to the cemetery, but she said that, if possible, she would like to stay with me and go to the cemetery with me instead of an official escort.

We talked and talked about Rolf. Then she said, "I've promised my husband that I would keep my eyes and ears open while I'm here so that I can tell him what's going on. I assume you know things we don't back home."

"We think the end of the war is near."

"The end of Germany?"

"Yes. The English will liberate us."

"Wouldn't the Russians make it here faster?"

"We don't like them."

"What will happen to the Germans here?"

I pointed at the kitchen knife. "Ten-year-old boys will stab them."

"We're hated to such a degree?"

Before I could catch myself, I was in tears. "I, myself, will kill eight. Three for the agony of being separated from my child and parents, and five for killing my two sisters, my brother, his wife, and their four-year-old little girl. Eight good people. Shall I tell you why my parents were deported and five were killed?"

"I know, Rolf told me."

"You know —?" I gasped.

She embraced me. "I want you to come to Germany and live with us. You'll be safe. This is what Rolf would have wanted."

Out of her arms, I bit my lips and looked at the ceiling. "There was another girl . . ." I said softly.

"He left you for her?"

"No. But he might have in the end."

"Tell me about it."

I told her.

She stroked my back. Very calmly she said: "Men at war — living from day to day — only what Rolf *felt* for you should have meaning for you. Why, even the letter we received after he was dead spoke only of his love for you." Her hands fumbled in her pocketbook and she got out a letter with Rolf's handwriting. It was dated two days before he had been murdered.

"I came here," she continued, "to bring you home. We have prepared Rolf's room for you."

I drew away from her gently. "I can't leave here," I said.

"Why not?"

"I have to remain near my own people."

"But you have nobody here."

"I musn't take the easy way out. I have to fight for my life like my father in the labor camp and all the others." I smiled at her. "I'll come to see you after the war," I said.

"But among us you have the best chance to survive," she pleaded.

The tone of her voice and the expression in her gray eyes were exactly the same as when Rolf had insisted upon my becoming a *Volksdeutsche.* It was as if Rolf were talking to me from the grave.

"Think it over," she said. "Take your time. I'll be here for another two days." She sighed, and abruptly changed the subject. "Have you heard of the gas chambers?" she asked.

"I have."

"A friend told my husband, but we could not believe it. It's unthinkable."

"Unthinkable, that's all? Aren't you horrified?"

"Are you saying it's true?"

"If I had proof that they exist, I'd go crazy. It is horrible enough to know that they shoot my people down, or starve them, or lock them up and make them work until they drop." Then I snapped at her: "Have they told you about *that* back home?"

She took my hand, looked straight into my eyes, and said: "We did not vote for Hitler. However, once he was in power, there was little people with our *Weltanschaung* could do."

"Why not?"

"My husband is a registered social democrat. He lost his job and we were grateful that he was not thrown into a concentration camp. Rolf shared my husband's ideology. There was *never* any danger that *he* would run with the Nazis. It's our younger son, Dietrich, who seems to have gone the other way . . . We're worried about him."

Her large blue-gray eyes wavered under my stare. And her hands disengaged themselves from mine. ". . . And now that Dietrich has heard that his beloved brother was murdered by the Polish underground —"

This irrevelant remark sounded as if from far away.

One of my hands clasped the other, and in a restrained voice I said: "That's what the Germans say, but it's not true that Rolf was murdered by the Polish underground."

"Who then?"

"I can't tell you. Not now."

"You must."

"I can't. The safety of others depend upon my silence. I promise that if I survive the war, we'll get together again and I'll tell you all I know. As of now, I do want you to know that because of this killing, twenty innocent Poles have been picked up in the street at random and taken hostage. They are to be shot at the Three Crosses Square as a reprisal measure. Ten for Rolf and ten for his interpreter. Before these men are led to their execution their mouths will be stuffed with a chemical that dries like cement so they won't be able to sing the Polish national hymn."

"Innocent people made hostages and shot?"

"The walls of Warsaw are bullet-ridden."

She could not believe it.

"I can take you to the Three Crosses Square and show you the list and the notice announcing the executions."

"Take me there.'

I took her to the photo equipment store and let her read the notice worded both in German and Polish, pasted to the brick wall.

EXECUTION

On July 27, at 11:45, two Germans were shot down at the Three Crosses Square by the Polish underground. In reprisal twenty Poles, as listed below, have been condemned to death by a firing squad. The execution will take place on August 3, at 11:45 A.M. at the Three Crosses Square.

Rolf's mother asked me to read aloud the twenty Polish names which she could not pronounce.

I did as she requested, pronouncing sharply each and every syllable.

When I had finished she began to cry. Then she pulled her shoulders up and said: "Please, take me to Rolf's superior."

"Now?"

"Now. No one shall die for my son!"

"You don't believe that the Gestapo will change their decree?"

"I am his mother!"

I knew that nothing would come of her intervention, but I said: "Let's go."

It was past office hours, but Kommissar Korben was still working, and this time he was available. He received us immediately, and expressed his sympathy to both Rolf's mother and me.

"I came to beg for clemency," Mrs. Rechter said.

"Clemency for whom?" *Kommissar* Korben asked dumbfounded.

"Clemency for the ten innocent Poles who are sentenced to die for my son."

A sour smile grew on his lips. His slanted eyes jerked toward me. "Innocent? Who told you such nonsense?" He turned to Mrs. Rechter. "You have been misinformed *Madame.* They are criminals already condemned to death by the law. They'll be shot in the street instead of in the prison courtyard. You must understand that the brazenness of those organized rebels defies all imagination. Can you imagine, Mrs. Rechter, they had the audacity to throw grenades at the tramways taking the mourners back from your son's funeral? Two dead and many wounded. They shoot down our boys like dogs. Little arrangements such as these street executions are an intimidation. You may be sure, we have never executed innocent men."

"I see," Mrs. Rechter said softly.

It was his word against mine.

Korben's restless hands relaxed. "How long do you intend to stay in Warsaw?" he asked.

"I have my return ticket for a day after tomorrow, I would like to take Miss Szarek along. Could you help me?"

"Miss Szarek can get a permit immediately." Korben pushed a button. Kruger came in and was told to make arrangements for me.

"I am not ready yet, Mrs. Rechter," I said.

"There's no harm in having a permit." she answered.

"It is a great honor for me to meet you. I've always held your son in great esteem. He was a fine man, I miss him." Korben rose and shook hands with us. "Don't forget to pick up his belongings. There are a few valuables. A motorcycle, two cameras, and a gold-watch. I wish you a very good trip, Mrs. Rechter, and you too, Miss Szarek. I'm sure you'll like it in Germany —"

"Thank you for everything, *Herr Kommissar.*" Mrs. Rechter said.

"Please let me know if there is anything we can do for you." *Kommissar* Korben had the last word.

34

The Polish uprising in Warsaw had started. I had received advance notice through Vaclava, but I didn't take it seriously. She had given me the same information three times and each time it had turned out to be a false alarm. However, I had advised Frania not to move from Konstancin, but I myself was almost too late to go there. We found out later that the train I had taken was the last one leaving Belvedere Station and that from that time on we in Konstancin would be cut off from Warsaw and the rest of the country.

Lonelier than ever, I approached the small gatehouse of the Wirtman estate. The barking dog reminded me of the time Rolf came here with me to allay the landlady's suspicion about Frania.

As then, Frania's landlord, Antony, stepped out to see what was the matter. "It started! It started!" he said to me jubilantly as he reached for my suitcase.

Inside, I found Jan who did not know as yet that he was stranded.

Antony, always hospitable, transferred his two teenaged daughters to the garage and gave their room to "Mister Engineer." I joined the two girls in the garage for Frania's room was too small for two beds. It took only a few days for me to get used to crossing the yard to the gatehouse where Mrs. Antony served our meals. The weather was good, and the cane gave me support over the unevenness and the stones on the ground. In the gatehouse of a neighboring estate, prayer gatherings were held for the freedom-fighters in Warsaw. Most of the local people attended, and Frania and I followed their example. The prayer sessions were led by Father Bensch, a stranded priest.

At forty, Father Bensch's hair was gray, as were his bushy eyebrows. His smile was lopsided on account of a triangular scar that cut across his cheek. His baritone voice reminded me of my father's.

At the end of one of the gatherings, I stepped up to him and asked if I could see him alone. He suggested that I come to Sunday Mass and that he would arrange to talk to me afterwards. The Mass would be held at the chapel of an old-age home for retired actors run by Franciscans.

On Sunday, the walk to the old-age home took me twenty minutes. The theme of Father Bensch's sermon was "Cleansing Through Suffering." The rhythm of his clear voice evoked my father's and, oddly enough, the little river in Niemirov where I had spent many happy childhood moments — swimming and floating on my back with my eyes on the sky which was deep blue, blue as nowhere else. Then, lying in the grass, letting my body dry in the sun. Twittering birds. The mild breezes, God's caresses.

Father Bensch stood before me. The room to which he had taken me looked out on a luxuriously green lawn that stretched all the way to the highway.

"What is bothering you, child?"

"I cannot forget the man I lost."

"Why should you forget him?"

"My friends say I should stop mourning and forget him."

"I'm sure your friends mean well, but why tear a beloved one from your heart only because his time on earth is up? Does remembering him give you comfort?"

"He was a good man."

"Then dwell on his goodness!"

I nodded.

"Think of him whenever you feel lonely and by all means wear mourning if that reflects your feelings."

"Father, he was not a Pole."

"You said he was a good man."

"He was a German."

He looked straight into my eyes. "Ye judge after flesh. I judge the man!"

In Warsaw the battle between Poles and Germans raged. We heard about Poles who barricaded themselves behind overturned tramways, many fighting with their bare hands. Tanks were captured and moved where they were needed by organizing religious processions so that women and children surrounded the tank holding up church banners and Saints as camouflage. Although their deception could be discovered at any moment, they walked securely singing litanies. Wherever the killing had thinned the lines of the resurgents, schoolboys filled in. They fought like men, they served as couriers, they built barricades and they dug ditches.

One day Antony came home in great excitement. "Take the binoculars," he said, "and come with me."

We followed him along a path which skirted the Wirtman estate fence and ran into a thinly wooded field. Antony's arm shot out toward the Vistula River. "There!" he said. "The Russians are in the suburbs, in Praga!"

We passed the binoculars from hand to hand, focusing on Russian soldiers shedding their uniforms and leaping into the water."

With the Red Army at Warsaw's threshold, our hopes for victory were substantiated. However, most Poles, dreading liberation by the Russians, kept praying that the final liberator would be the British. For the few Jews left, however, it mattered little who would be the liberator, and they counted the moments till the time when the Russians would come across the Kierbiedzia Bridge.

Since it was forbidden to own a radio, the fragments of news we received during the sixty-three days while Warsaw stood up against the Germans came through Father Bensch who was in touch with the underground of Konstancin. He would often find me eagerly waiting for him at the gate of the Wirtman Estate. I cherished the daily conversations with him.

When I first came to Antony's house, I was the only one who had money and provided support Frania and Jan as well. Later, when I became sensitive to what they might be feeling I changed the arrangement. Instead of paying Antony for their rooms and meals, I gave Frania a larger amount of money and made loans to Jan which he would pay back when he returned to Rava-Ruska. But he needed more money every day. Although far from being a drunkard, he liked his bottle of vodka and enjoyed joining the men at the local bar.

Jan criticized whatever I did. Trying to please "Mr.

Engineer," whom he was proud to have in his house, Antony supported him. Frania on the other hand never stood up for me so I was alone.

Jan referred to me as "Limpy" which was strange since he himself was slightly lame. Perhaps he sensed my resentment of how much of my money he spent. He ridiculed my friendship with Father Bensch. "You should see yourself," he said. "You and that priest of yours shuffling along in his torn shoes. What do you see in him?"

"He is the best."

"How many priests have you known?" he grinned.

Even this allusion to my religion did not crack Frania's loyalty in her man. She said nothing. Perhaps she was afraid of him?

"Father Bensch is stranded here. I wonder if he can even afford a hot meal. He asks for nothing but gives all he can to everybody."

"Who is all, you? We — Frania and I and Antony, his family, and many others — consider Father Szarejko far superior. That seems to be the opinion of the whole community because he has better income."

"Father Szarejko has a parish here," I said. "But Father Bensch is more than a shepherd, he's an apostle."

Jan broke into derisive laughter and Frania, who had become his echo, chimed in.

I went to the garage and sat there brooding.

Later, outside at the gate, I saw Father Bensch coming down the dirt road.

This time the news was that evacuees from a Warsaw hospital had been put up in Konstancin, at villa Vera. I could hardly wait for the morning to visit them. Perhaps one of the patients would know something about my friends, friends with whom I could talk about Rolf.

35

The town was not yet awake when I made my way through the fog to villa Vera. Somewhere a dog barked. Here and there smoke, spiraling from a chimney, melted in the mist. Turning a corner from the Main Street, I collided with a chimneysweep. Although I would have denied that I believed in the superstition that this brings luck, I touched him. Then I went on only to bump into somebody once again; this time with a German. "Oh, *Verzeihung* (pardon me)," he stammered.

"*Przepraszam bardzo* (forgive me)," I gasped.

Finding his bearings, he barked at me, "Papers!" He gave them a glance and let me go.

Villa Vera loomed in the fog with startling suddeness. I passed through the gate and found a beehive of activity. Crates and bundles were being carried to the house. Nurses were tending the wounded, who sat in groups of three and four in the garden.

I stepped up to three men and asked whether they were from Chmielna or Szopena Street. They shook their heads and suggested that I inquire among the sick inside.

Berler's living room, where thirteen employees of Vinetta had had their Christmas dinner, was now a hospital for the critically ill. I went from bed to bed looking for a face I knew. When I was about to give up, a man called my name.

"You know me?" I asked the emaciated young stranger. "Did you live on Chmielna Street, Szopena or Mazowiecka Street? Do you happen to know Maria Lasocka, Vaclava Gorski, or Zosia Szarbecka . . .?"

147

Impatiently the man shook his head and gestured for me to come closer. "I've seen you with Mr. Rechter."

I was shocked.

"Sit down," the man said.

I sat down on the edge of his bed. "Did you know Mr. Rechter?"

"As a matter of fact I knew him very well."

"How was that?"

"I am a detective . . ." he paused.

"Well —"

"Occasionally I worked with him. In fact, I was with him when he was murdered."

I caught my breath.

"That's when I was wounded. My heart, my lungs, both kidneys . . . They have operated on me again and again, but they can't fool me. Mr. Rechter was lucky to have been spared what I've been through. I envy him."

Talking exhausted him.

"Can I be of any help to you?" I leaned closer.

"There's something I must tell you before I die," he whispered and closed his eyelids which were almost transparent. He seemed to have fallen asleep.

I drew the blanket around his shoulders and remained sitting, waiting.

After some time, he awoke moaning, his face distorted with pain. He opened his eyes and beckoned me closer. "Promise me that you won't tell anyone," he demanded in a low rasping voice.

"I promise."

"Cross yourself."

I made the sign of the cross.

"My name is Boryn, Detective Boryn. I knew what Mr. Rechter was up to. He was giving the Polish underground weapons — all kinds of permits, he manipulated dossiers. The fool even helped the Jews."

I made myself shrug.

"But he didn't know that the Gestapo were watching and that his informers were rewarded." A dry wheezing cough shook his frail body.

"Why didn't they arrest him?" I asked.

"Prosecuting Rechter the legal way would have stirred up too much dust, understand?" The ghost of a smile touched his withered lips. "So — they killed him. They killed those they had put to spy on him, too, understand?" He struggled for breath. "I'm frightened," he whispered.

Was he one of the informers? Or was he frightened that once the Germans were gone, he'd have to answer to the Polish underground for Rolf's death? Something about the man was repulsive. I wanted to leave, but he gripped my arm. "Help me," he whimpered.

"Shall I send you a priest?"

I saw terror in his eyes. Then he covered them with his hands.

Two weeks went by. One day Father Bensch asked me, "Have you seen Boryn lately?"

"No."

"You could help a dying man."

"No."

"He is repenting."

"He was an informer."

"He needs your charity."

"I am not that good by nature."

The priest raised his bushy eyebrows. "Most of us are not good by nature. But we should struggle against this natural inclination. It's hard . . ."

"He may have been the one who delivered the man I loved to the Gestapo."

"If you believe that then only you can absolve him."

"Has he confessed?"

His shocked glance put me in my place. He excused himself and left.

The uprising came to an end. The freedom fighters could fight no longer and were forced to agree to have the entire population of Warsaw evacuated to villages. Then the Germans went from one building to another and in a well-ordered manner burned the capital of Poland to the ground.

36

The soldier whipped the horse and we moved off.

I glanced at the gate where Frania and Jan were standing, holding hands. The wagon went around a corner and rattled along the open road. Only half an hour ago we had been sitting calmly around the lunch table. Not even the knock at the door had startled us. For hope was high, the end of the war was near.

Upon entering, the German snapped: "Lieutenant Kuntze. Which one is *Fraulein* Szarek?"

Automatically I handed him my *Kennkarte*.

"The *Ortskommandantur* (Military Town Administration) in Piaseczno has appointed you their interpreter," the lieutenant said.

"Me? I am not very good at it."

"You leave that decision to us," he snapped. "You are to come with me immediately."

"But —"

"Take only enough for a few days. Your baggage will be picked up some other time."

"Come with me to Warsaw," Fischer said. "I am going for business by car. Come with me. You don't need any luggage. I will bring your belongings some other time."

"When are you going?"

150

"In three days."

"I can't. I have to go to Zloczov."

"You can go to Zloczov tomorrow and come back the day after. Do you want to take Bruno along?"

"Would you take him, too?"

"Of course!"

I hugged him.

Life in the streets of Zloczov seemed peacful. On Mickevicza Street where my in-laws lived I noticed the quiet and the cleanliness and could not help but compare it with the deafening noise of traffic in Lvov.

Neither Mark's warm welcome nor Suzan's icy stare while Mark and I exchanged news awoke any reaction in me. Anyway, Bruno was the main object of attention and affection for both of them.

When we had a few minutes alone I told Mark of my plan to go to Warsaw and there to register with the police under an assumed name.

"It sounds like a thriller . . ." he said.

"Today it may seem fantastic, but tomorrow other people will be doing the same thing. In fact you should do it too, Mark."

"I'll think of it," he said smiling superciliously.

"I noticed an almost imperceptible tic in his right cheek.

At the dinner table Suzan said: "Mark told me you have some wild scheme about taking Bruno to Warsaw. But he's decided not to let him go with you."

"What?" I turned to Mark.

"If you want to go to Warsaw, go ahead," Suzan continued. "Go to Honolulu if you like. But Mark will not let you take a four-year-old child into such an adventure."

I gritted my teeth. "This 'adventure' as you call it, may save Bruno's life." I said, my eyes fixed on Mark.

"Do you have an apartment, even a room in Warsaw?" Suzan asked.

"I have nothing."

"Then you can't take the child now," she said firmly, as if that settled the mater.

Willing with all my might for Mark to look at me I said: "Well, why don't you speak?"

He raised his eyes from his plate. "Suzan is probably right," he said, and gave me a glance and then looked down at his plate again.

His total surrender to his older sister added another layer to the contempt I realized I had been feeling for him for a long time.

Repressing my disgust I tried as objectively as possible to size up the situation. I was determined to keep my control. I had to make a cool appraisal of the situation and to see what I could do to keep my child with me. I put my elbows on the table and leaned across towards Mark.

"Mark, with your knowledge of Polish and with your 'Gentile' appearance you run little risk of being recognized as a Jew. You always wanted to assimilate with the Poles, now is your chance. Buy forged papers as I did and come with us to Warsaw."

Mark played with the teaspoon and then took his glass to his mouth, evidently unaware there was no more tea in it.

A feeling of exasperation and anger rose in me. "Well," I said. Mark looked at his sister again.

I felt the blood rush to my face. I turned to Suzan: "What is this about Mark's decision to keep Bruno here? Was it his decision or yours?"

She stared back at me without answering.

I could feel my cheeks burning. "I am fed up with your interference in business which is strictly between me and him," I shouted, my control finally gone.

"Quiet," she said. "I can hear you without your screaming at me. You will wake Bruno." She pushed her chair back from the table. I will not take any further abuse from a person like you." she said in an icy tone, and strode majestically out of the dining room into the kitchen.

It was the first time I had faced up to her, and a sense of relief and freedom surged through me. I turned to Mark breathlessly: "You're afraid of her," I sneered. "You can't stand up to her even when your child's welfare is at stake."

The door from the kitchen to the foyer slammed and I realized that Suzan had been listening on the other side of the door.

In my lap my hands clenched into fists. "Damn her," I said. "Damn her to hell!"

Mark was playing with crumbs of bread. He raised his head and without looking at me said slowly: "She loves Bruno very much. She really does —"

I suddenly noticed that the fingers rolling bits of bread into grey pellets on the white tablecloth trembled. I looked closely at Mark. His skin had a yellowish unhealthy cast and on his right cheek there was that tic. In a flash my anger drained away. I bit my lips. "Are you all right, Mark?" I asked quietly.

He nodded.

"You're sure —?" I said.

He nodded again. "Listen," he said, "maybe it's not such a bad idea to leave Bruno with us until you get yourself registered with the police and settled in Warsaw? You will be free to move around and get things done without the burden of child. Doesn't that make sense, Roma?" Now he faced me.

"Maybe."

"And after you've made all the arrangements, like finding a trustworthy Catholic to take Bruno in board, you can let me know by telegram and we can meet in Lvov." He sighed. "It will be too dangerous to come to Zloczov without your armband. People might recognize you."

"Perhaps we should find out how Bruno feels about my leaving him," I said.

"Don't worry about that. It won't be the first time. You know he feels at home here and is happy with us. Well?" he smiled, making the tic in his cheek more prominent. "What do you say, Roma, agreed?"

I shrugged my shoulders.

"Is it settled then?" he persisted. "You send a telegram and I bring Bruno to Lvov."

"Will Suzan let you?" I asked, my voice strident again.

"Suzan loves the child. She wants the best for him too. You know that. We will be there, I promise!"

"I haven't made up my mind yet," I said.

However, after a sleepless night of weighing the pros and cons of the situation I had to admit that it would be better if I could bring Bruno to Warsaw when a home had already been set up for him.

We made the twenty kilometers to Piaseczno in about an hour. At the *Ortskommandantur*, Lieutenant Kuntze handed me over to Sergeant Brucke who led me past a long line of Polish petitioners in the first large room to a door bearing the sign: *Kommandant* Schellberg. Sergeant Brucke tugged at his uniform, adjusted his tie, straightened his shoulders, and knocked softly.

The sergeant opened the door, gestured to me to follow him inside, saluted, and clicked his heels, "The interpreter, *Herr Kommandant*," he announced. "The name is Szarek."

After I had been looked over by the *Kommandant,* Sergeant Brucke took me out again and told me about my duties. I was to assist in the communication between German officials and Polish petitioners who came to apply for travel permits. As a rule such permits were not difficult to obtain except for traveling to Warsaw. I was to interpret for evacuees from Warsaw who came to apply for rooms or to locate relatives from whom they had become separated. Parcels for husbands and sons in German labor camps had to be shipped through the *Ortskommandantur* and more often than not it was necesary to re-pack and re-address them.

The living quarters assigned me in the house of a Polish family were sumptuous compared to the Antonys' garage. There was a rug, pictures on the walls, and curtains on the windows. I had a real bed instead of a cot, and a full-length mirror was attached to the outside of the wooden closet door. It was hard for me to look at myself with my ever-present cane.

There was no guard. I decided to run away. But I needed help, and I thought of Father Bensch.

On Sunday, my day off, I walked twenty kilometers to the old-age home in Skolimov. The trees along the road were golden in the bright autumn sun. Church bells were ringing calling the parishioners to Sunday service.

When Father Bensch left the chapel, he found me waiting. He knew I had been "kidnapped" by the *Ortskommandantur* and showered me with questions. In the end, to my surprise, he discouraged me from running away. According to him I was now in a position where there would be many opportunities to help my fellow-countrymen.

Then he asked me to the rectory and handed me a book written in German, suggesting that I use my free time to translate it into Polish. The title, *Menschen die zur Kirche kamen* (people who converted) roused my interest. I glanced at the preface and noticed the list of twelve celebreties who had converted to Catholicism. I felt myself blush. Had he guessed that I was Jewish? Had I given myself away in the quiet hours when he spoke to me about his religious philosophy?

"I wouldn't want us to lose touch, Father," I said. "Your guidance has been precious to me."

"We'll never lose touch with each other, unless you want to," he said, handing me a slip of paper. "You can write to this address should we become separated. I used to teach Canonic Law at the Lublin Catholic University and hope to do so again. You'll be able to reach me through the Dean's office." He took my hand between his. "Stay where God puts you, child."

Then he told me of a typewriter that had been requisitioned from the old-age home by the *Ortskommandantur.* It had belonged to an old actor who now, deprived of the means he used to write his memoirs, was noticeably deteriorating.

Throughout the following week I worked at softening Sergeant Brucke with flattery and dropped remarks about the deplorable condition of that particular typewriter. Finally he agreed that it was only in the way and should be returned to where it had come from.

Father Bensch beamed.

But I did not. What a tactician I was where my own interests were not at stake! I reproached myself for not having been equally insistent that Bruno come with me, equally insistent that Rolf go into hiding after his first hearing at the Gestapo, or after those shots missed us by inches at the theatre.

Overnight the walls of the buildings in Piaseczno were plastered with posters inviting Poles to join the German army. They were promised fast promotion and lucrative financial benefits for the families they would leave behind.

Lieutenant Kuntze organized a recruiting station in the building of the *Ortskommandantur.*

But I heard him mutter to Brucke, "This is a waste of time. Nobody will show up."

To the surprise of both of us, soon some young boys were shyly circling the station. Some did sign up for duty. For the most part they were poor Ukrainians seeking a way out of hunger and cold. Kuntze registered about thirty boys daily. Until they were transported to a military camp, they were the responsibility of the *Ortskommandantur* and our cook, Stella, had a difficult time feeding the starved youngsters.

After the last volunteers were shipped off, a German military unit arrived in town, sealed off the streets, and raided apartments. They rounded up men, regardless of age, to send to labor camps.

While this speedy and skillfully organized *Action* went on, a Polish woman came to my desk demanding to see the *Kommandant.* I took her to him.

"Whenever you called upon my husband to do a job," she said in broken German, "he obeyed. Now they took him. Is this his reward? How am I supposed to support my six children?"

"It's not my fault, I have no jursidiction over this *Action,*" the *Kommandant* said in a soft voice I had never heard before. "Cecylia," he turned to me, "take down the man's name."

The woman switched to Polish and said to me: "Will he let my husband go? In the name of Jesus Christ, help me!"

Brucke shoved her out.

"Herr Kommandant," I said, "after this raid you'll have more enemies among the towns-people. The Poles that weren't rounded up this time know they will be the next time. They know they'll be sent off to amunition factories in Germany which might be bombed. So, they run to the woods. That's how the partisans grow — day by day —" I stopped, afraid I had already dared say too much.

"The Poles can't blame me for what others are doing."

"They don't know the difference between one German unit and another. Those who directed the *Action* will soon be far away and those remaining here will become the target of terror. I hate to think of our rides to villages in your district with partisans hiding in the woods. Perhaps you could tell your superior how difficult it has become."

"It's good thinking, Cecylia. I must admit, it's good thinking. Brucke! *Zum Teufel noch einmal* (Damn it)! Brucke! Where is Brucke?"

Sergeant Brucke was clicking his heels and now stood at attention.

"Brucke, take Cecylia and get to that assembly place. Make it fast. Have this Ba . . . Bar . . . what's his name, released. Cecylia, you have his name on a paper."

I gave it to him.

The *Kommandant* wrote a few words on a form, copied the Polish name, stamped it and gave it to Brucke.

Within half an hour Baranovski, the woman's husband, was home.

The news traveled fast.

Within an hour the office was flooded with women begging for the release of a husband, son, or brother.

Half his hand hidden in his uniform jacket, the *Kommandant* paced the floor, thinking. Abruptly, he pushed through the throng of Polish women, stepped into his office, gave orders to be left undisturbed, and slammed the door shut.

After a few minutes of quiet, the *Kommandant's* voice was heard from behind the door. It swelled to a roar. "The people run to the woods! I cannot keep order in town! No, no, I say, you have no right to interfere in my territory. I'll file complaints . . . *Himmel! Donner Wetter!* Don't you understand German? I'm telling you, it's the last time!"

He came out, his face redder, his voice hoarse. "Lieutenant Kuntze, I want you to take a message to the assembly place. Any Pole with a Piaseczno stamp on his identification card is to be released. Pass on the message giving my verbal authorization to the captain in charge and to no one else." The *Kommandant* raised himself to whisper the secret code of authorization in Kuntze's ear.

Later that day most of the men caught in the raid were released and the Piaseczno population was jubilant.

"Don't run. Stay where God puts you." Father Bensch's words echoed in my mind.

37

A few weeks later, I went to visit Frania and was surprised to find Jan still there. "The way to Rava-Ruska is now open," I told Jan.

"His decisions are none of your business," Frania said.

I asked her for the cooker that I had left in her custody and took out a few gold coins to cover her needs for a long time. If she wanted to share them with someone else, that was her business.

On my way back to Piaseczno, my thoughts wandered to the friends I had had when Rolf and I had been together. Maria, Zosia, Vaclava, where could they be? Had they survived the bloodshed in Warsaw? If they did, were they near or far away? Would I find them again?

I thought of Stella, the petite, redheaded, young woman who was the chef in the kitchen of the *Ortskommandantur*. I had grown to like her although so far we had exchanged only an occasional few words. I sympathized with her each time the *Kommandant* sent me to her with complaints: The chicken was too dry, the soup too thin, the steak too well done, the potatoes too hard, the butter not fresh enough or the coffee not hot enough.

On the spur of the moment I decided to pay Stella a visit.

I found her ironing her only blouse. She explained that she had to wash the blouse and her only slip every day after coming home from work and usually did the ironing the following morning, but that on Sunday she did both the same day.

I was surprised to see a child's folded shirt and learned that

158

she had a six-year-old boy. Her extreme poverty was obvious. She had been able to conceal it from me at work for she had always been neatly dressed, her red hair impeccably brushed up in a plain knot. Only now did I remember that she had worn the white pinstriped percale blouse every single day.

In my mind I selected a few things I could easily do without. But how could I give them to her without hurting her pride?

She seemed very glad to see me and admitted that she, too, had been looking for an opportunity to become friends.

I asked Stella who was taking care of her child while she was at work.

"The landlady," Stella said pouring tea.

Stella and I liked each other immediately.

When missing Rolf became unbearable and I had an urge at least to see my sister, the thought that Stella would welcome me at any time provided the willpower to leave Frania to her own life.

On Sunday morning I usually went to the chapel of the old-age home where I listened to Father Bensch's sermons. A sense of peace would come over me. His voice became my father's, asking me to judge Frania with charity.

Sunday was the day I found a link between myself and the strange world around me, a world without Rolf.

38

"**M**iss Szarek!" the *Kommandant* roared.

I sprang to attention on the instant, as did everybody in response to his voice.

"Our unit is going west," he informed me when I entered his office. "Be in readiness."

Three days later the forty Germans of the Piaseczno *Ortskommandantur* boarded a special train together with their twelve Polish employees. The Germans traveled in the coaches, and the civilians were stowed away in a cattle car together with crates and boxes.

The trip to Szydloviec took several days because of interruptions and delays. Often the train stood motionless for hours on an open track.

In Szydloviec we moved into the school building from which the previous *Ortskommandantur* had moved on farther west. The upper floor included the apartment of the schoolmistress whom Schellberg promptly evicted. Seeing how upset she was I suggested to the *Kommandant* that having her in the house might be a safeguard against sabotage.

"Good thinking, good thinking, Cecylia," the *Kommandant* said, and consented to let her stay.

The grateful schoolmistress offered me one room of her rooms but I gave it to Stella so that she could be near her child while at work downstairs. I moved into the room which had been assigned to her in an apartment house a few blocks away. However, I had to share it with a Polish waitress, another employee of the *Ortskommandantur.*

Once I had to accompany the *Kommandant* to an orphanage run by nuns. He told the Mother Superior that they would have to vacate the premises within ten days to make room for a soldier's rest camp.

To my question as to where she planned to place the sixty children, she answered: "The Lord will provide."

The *Kommandant* said that he would have the local police order each childless family in the village to take one or two orphans.

It meant friends would be separated; it meant strange surroundings; it meant some children would be placed with people who did not really want them. I mentioned this to the *Kommandant.*

"War is war," he answered shortly. "I don't want to hear another word."

After work I went upstairs to see the schoolmistress and told her what happened. She said there was a castle on the outskirts of Szydloviec and perhaps when the *Kommandant* was in a good mood, he could be convinced that the castle was a better, or, at least, an equally good location for a soldier's rest home.

I knocked at the *Kommandant's* door and told him about this new possibility for a rest home.

"What sort of a castle?"

"A beautiful seventeenth century building that belonged to a Polish duke. It stands in the midst of a magnificent park. I think it's much more suitable than that orphanage. It's just ideal for a rest camp."

"Did you see it?"

"Of course," I lied. "A local pointed it out as a tourist attraction. They don't want to be known only for the manufacture of barrels. They're proud of their castle."

The *Kommandant* opened the door and roared: "Brucke! Have them harness up, I'm leaving. Szarek, you're coming along!"

The Mother Superior who came to the *Ortskommandantur* to express her gratitude for the canceled evacuation order, stopped upon leaving the *Kommandant's* office at my desk. "You see how the Lord provided?" she said. And she slipped a Saint Antony amulet into my hand. "He will always protect you."

39

Bruno appeared to me in my dreams as he had before, but now Rolf was sometimes at his side. I dreaded to see them together for I wanted to believe that my little boy was still alive, taken care of by a Polish family. My outcries awakened the waitress and I started to worry that perhaps I might betray myself and say somehing compromising during my sleep. After that I kept myself awake for hours.

One evening, before my roommate came home, a letter was pushed under the door. It read:

Dziewczyno (girl)!

A Polish girl should refuse to work for the Germans. Leave your job at once or you will have your head shaved or worse . . .

The underground

Of all things! I was so angry I was ready to dash out to find the underground and let them know that I was one of them. But I realized that I had no proof, unless Vaclava were here in Szydloviec. Without proof, the local people might expose me to the *Ortskommandant* and any kind of investigation would be dangerous. Who could help me? Rolf, my protector, was dead. Fischer, my good adviser, arrested, probably deported. The only person I could *perhaps* trust was Stella.

Usually I hurried along the twisting corridor leading to the exit with fingers holding my nose against the heavy stench of urine. Today, I peered right and left into every corner in fear of a lurking underground man with a pair of scissors in his hand. When I reached the exit door, I leapt outside and made a run for the schoolmistress' apartment.

Stella welcomed me, drying her hands. I let her read the note. "Threatened by the underground? You of all people?" She looked at me aghast. "Don't they know what you are doing for the Poles? Isn't it common knowledge about the orphans? Don't they know how many sons and husbands were exempt from forced labor in Germany on account of you?"

"Perhaps one refusal earns more bitterness than all favors added up bring gratitude."

"I still think it was a mistake."

"I wish it was."

"Why do you think the note was addressed to you? Perhaps it was meant for the waitress."

"I'm sure they pushed the letter under the door when they knew I was alone. Stella, what am I to do?"

"Ask the *Kommandant* to fire you."

"I've tried that before. He won't let me go. Maybe the nuns or the schoolmistress know a contact in the underground. They could let them know that I'm not a collaborator. Please, Stella, you go —"

Stella looked away. "I don't know," she said. "The schoolmistress is an odd person . . ."

"Then go to the nuns for me. I'd go myself, but I'm afraid to be out on the highway or in the woods."

"How would the Mother Superior have contact with the underground —?"

It was clear that she was making excuses. Perhaps since she, too, was a Pole working for the Germans, she had reason to be afraid of the same repercussions? "Stella, I don't think you have to be afraid. The underground threatened me, the only Polish office worker. They have not threatened any of the household staff."

"I'll go to the *Kommandant*. You wait here," she said, and was gone.

I watched Andrzej put his toys away — yarn spools which Stella had collected for him. Then he started to undress.

"Shall I help you?" I asked.

"No!" he said. "Mama said I must never let anybody undress me. I am a big boy." He took off his shirt first and slipped into his long nightgown before dropping his trousers. Then he got into bed, turned to the wall, pulled the blanket over his head, and did not make another move.

Soon Stella returned. "The *Kommandant* said not to worry, he'll take care of everything. I suggest you stay here overnight. Andrzej will sleep with me."

I told her how bashfully her son had undressed under his nightgown.

Stella blushed a scarlet color.

Suddenly I understood.

"Stella," I exclaimed, and then hesitated. What if I were wrong? No. Stella's face, the typical face of a redheaded Polish girl, all at once showed the intangible characteristics of a redheaded Jewish girl. "Stella —" I said gently, reaching for her hand. "Both of us have an ancestor by the name of — of Moses."

Stella stared at me. "You . . ? Impossible!"

"Yes, Stella, I am also a daughter of Israel."

We embraced; we hugged.

Stella began to cry softly.

It was very late when she moved sleeping Andrzej into her bed and I slipped into his.

I tossed and turned, kept awake by the aroma that emanated from Andrzej's pillow, the peculiar sweet scent of a little boy's hair.

Next morning, I found the streets plastered with notices reading:

> Our interpreter who is of Polish nationality has been hired for the sole purpose of establishing better relations between the Polish people and the German Occupying Forces. Attempts have been made to intimidate her. If she, or any other employee of this outpost should be harmed in any way whatsoever, ten Polish citizens will be shot to death in reprisal.
>
> *Stadtkommandant* Schellberg

I hurried to the *Kommandant*. "Have you seen the dispatch?" he boasted before I had a chance to say good morning. "Marvelous idea, wasn't it?"

"It will stir up more resentment," I said. "Please — The problem can be solved by quietly replacing me. I'll be glad to stay long enough to break in a new interpreter."

"How many times do I have to repeat it? I won't let you go. Nor will I let Stella go, nor the others who are good workers. Even

back in Germany we'll need people like you. I will not let a conquered people bully me."

"Please, I'm so frightened."

"And encourage them to threaten us? Never! Otherwise
they'll frighten away all my workers."

From then on I would be scared to walk to and from work. But
two days later, good news came my way. The schoolmistress told
Stella that the Russians had launched a gigantic offensive and
that the Germans were retreating along the entire front. That
meant that the end of the war had come closer.

The *Kommandant* set up barricades on the streets. He had
only forty men under his command. Each time he inspected the
barricades, he found something to complain about. He called it
outright sabotage, made the local mayor responsible, and instructed to get the message across to the Polish workmen that they
would be deported if the barricades were not in perfect order by
the end of the week.

Christmas was near.

I was given the task of wrapping the small gifts the *Kommandant* had prepared for the staff and he told me to compose little
rhymes which would make small allusion to the recipient. The
Christmas Eve at Berler's made me look forward to the celebration. I became happy at the thought of the beautiful tree I had
helped to decorate, the festive table at which I had been a partici-
pant, and the mood of reverence and warmth which, in spite of the
war, had carried the message of universal peace and good-will.

Now Berler was dead. And the thirteen imposters, who had
been invited to his table — where were they?

For the first time the civilian workers were invited into the
German dining room for the roast goose dinner Stella had
prepared for all of us, although the separation between the Poles
and the Germans was preserved with me as the link between the
two, the "Pole" of the highest rank, in her best dress, sitting beside
the German of lowest rank.

The *Kommandant's* toast was followed by the singing of
Silent Night, Holy Night. German words mingled with Polish.
During this the *Kommandant* sat with his lips closed and his expression grim, fiddling with a red apple. Suddenly, his mouth
opened wide and in a coarse tone of voice he burst out: *Oh Suzanna, Das Leben Ist Nicht Schwer, Die Allerbeste Braut Des Krieges
Ist Das Gewehr* (Oh Suzanna, life is a trifle, the greatest bride of

war is the rifle), rhythmically banging on the table, alternating elbow and fist, elbow and fist. The tone of voice, the libretto of the military march-song sounded so obscene that there was shocked silence. Then Sergeant Brucke obediently fell in with the *Kommandant* and he nodded at the others to join in as well.

The *Kommandant* saw the tears in my eyes and, challenged by him, I explained that I was a little homesick, like all of us probably were. The drunken eyes of Lieutenant Kuntze that had been making an effort to focus on me, were now also moist with tears. Perhaps it was this moment of communion that led him to confide in me later that the *Ortskommandantur* was to move west again at any moment and that the staff would definitely be taken along.

40

That the front had moved closer to Szydloviec was now accepted by everyone. The castle, at first transformed by the *Kommandant* into a rest home for convalescing soldiers, had now become a hospital, occupied only by serious casualties. A few were lucky enough to be transported to Germany. The rest waited for surgeons to arrive.

Soldiers who had been separated from their units came to the *Ortskommandantur,* to register so that they would not be accused of desertion. They expressed their surprise that they should find a German outpost so close to the battlefield.

The *Kommandant* assured the exhausted men that a turn of the tide was imminent and that what looked like a retreat was really an evacuation of German forces from territory which would be struck by a new secret weapon. "It's something staggering. I heard the *Fuhrer* himself say it on my last furlough in Germany. This secret weapon will bring the whole world to its knees!"

It sounded convincing.

Only a few days later, Kuntze stormed out from the *Kommandant's* office with an order that I should get the railroad station on the phone. The station did not answer. I told the operator that this was impossible, that somebody must be there, that she should go on ringing.

The station, however, could not be contacted.

A furious *Kommandant* ordered Kuntze to get out a horse and

167

got to the station himself. Kuntze returned to report that the depot was deserted.

The *Kommandant's* red face turned ashen. After a few minutes of thought he shouted an order to confiscate forty horses and twenty sleds and then barked at me to be at the office in an hour with my belongings.

Upstairs in Stella's room both of us were in a state of high tension as we discussed how we could slip away, but when we opened the door we found a soldier on guard. "I'll take your luggage down," he said.

In the office we waited another hour.

Sleds were lined up outside. Plain, flat-bottomed farmers' sleds, built like their wagons except that they were equipped with runners instead of wheels. It took another two hours before the sleds were loaded and could leave.

The retreat from Szydloviec had begun.

It was camouflaged by the dark of night. Just as the German staff of the railroad station had left without giving a thought to the *Ortskommandantur,* the *Ortskommandant* left without concerning himself about the wounded in the castle.

On the sled, Stella, Andrzej, and I huddled close together in the straw for warmth. We did not utter a word. Behind us, Sergeant Brucke and a soldier were sitting on my trunk between bundles of bedding, Stella's suitcase, a basket containing the *Ortskommandantur's* silver cutlery, and two sacks of fodder for the horse. In front of us, in the driver's seat, was Kuntze who was in charge of the sleds and jumped off from time to time to make sure everything was all right.

We glided through the snow, white fields on both sides of the road alternating with stretches of forest. I dozed off.

The sound of voices awakened me at dawn. We were at an intersection with a main road, which was jammed by sleds, cars, motorcycles, and soldiers on foot. We had to stop. Whistling, the Military Police tried to impose order, seeing that vehicles belonging to one unit remained together. It took several hours before our unit was given the signal to move into the main road. Whenever we came to a village, Stella and I were tempted to jump off.

Suddenly Kuntze blew his whistle. His sleds halted, "To the ditches!" he shouted.

Only then did I hear the rumble of planes. With the help of my cane, I struggled out of the sled and limped along following Stella and Andrzej as quickly as I could. We lay face down at the roadside amongst the soldiers and covered our heads with our hands, and the next moment the bombers were over us. The noise was earshattering. Then quickly it faded away. I sat up and looked around. I saw soldiers with faces as pale as ours. For the first time I saw Germans frightened to death. It gave me satisfaction.

Sergeant Brucke helped us up into the sled. Stella and I rebuilt our nest of straw and blankets and made Andrzej lie down across our laps so that he might continue his interrupted afternoon nap.

The following day, more alert, we heard a faint buzzing from far away. Then we saw six dark points, like birds, flying in our direction. All along the line of sleds soldiers were leaping to the road. Stella and I with Andrzej dangling between us rushed as fast as my limp allowed for a nearby clump of trees. There, I threw Andrzej to the ground and myself on top of him like Rolf had done in Vaclava's basement.

Already the planes were overhead. With a terrible screech they dove toward us, shooting, and then swooped away roaring upward. I peeked through my arms and saw them circling now.

"They'll dive again," Stella screamed. "We won't get out of this."

"It wouldn't be the worst way to die," I answered.

"I want Mama to live," Andrzej piped from under me. Then I heard him pray: "Jesusenko, protect my mama."

Once again the planes tilted and fell into their whistling descent. Once again we covered our heads, listening while holding our breath. With the sudden explosion of the machine guns, I pressed my face deeper into the snow.

Stella prayed. She shouted the words as if God could not hear them in all this deafening noise. I found myself whimpering for my father. Did he pray for me three times daily as he had promised? I fumbled in my coat pocket to touch the medal the Mother Superior had given me. "Dear God, let at least this child live!"

The planes were now ascending.

But circling a few times they dived again. Again came the hail of bullets. Again the roar of ascent. Then the noise began to fade.

"Move," Andrzej said, poking at me. "I can't breathe."

Thank heaven the child was alive! Sliding off Andrzej, I glanced in Stella's direction. She, too, was all right. I sat up and reached for my cane beside me and, supporting myself against the birch behind me, got to my feet.

Now I looked around. A soldier nearby who was sitting in the snow touched his leg and his hand came away red with blood. Behind him two soldiers lay face up, dead. Farther away I saw the *Kommandant* weaving his way among the trees, bending down, straightening up, walking on. He was counting his dead and wounded.

"He has no right to drag my child any farther," Stella said. "As a matter of fact what right does he have to force civilians to travel with a military unit that is under fire every few hours. Come on, let's tell him that we've had it."

We waited until he was through with his inspection and then we approached him. In answer to our complaints the *Kommandant* told us that there was no place we could go to. We were surrounded by Russians. And, slapping his holster, he concluded in a reassuring voice: "Don't worry, I'll never let you fall into *their* hands. If worse comes to worst, there is a bullet for each of you, and of course, one for myself."

We went back to our sled.

Later in the day one of the sled horses behind us refused to take another step. The entire line of sleds was stopped.

The rebellious horse was examined, patted, shouted at, and finally whipped. The horse neighed, and eyes wild, started off in a frantic zigzagging trail until the sled finally capsized and the crates and sacks of fodder and wounded soldiers tumbled out into the snow. Once again the horse, bracing its legs, refused to move in any direction.

The *Kommandant* ordered Kuntze to load the wounded soldiers on the eight sleds parked ahead of the wretched horse, and take off for the next village. He would follow as soon as possible with the remaining twelve sleds.

As we glided from the scene of the disaster and from the *Kommandant's* pistol, I had a premonition that our fate had taken a favorable turn. At the outskirts of the next village Kuntze called for a halt at a farm. Vehicles of another unit were already parked there.

After four days and nights out in the open we had a fierce desire to get into the warmth of a house.

Holding on to the large pigskin pocketbook containing the electric cooker which served as a strongbox, I followed Stella and Andrzej into the large smoke-filled farm kitchen. It was crowded with German soldiers, some sitting on the floor, some around the stove, brooding. Three snoring soldiers, fully dressed, were lying on a bed. I would have given anything for a place on that bed to rest my hurting leg, but there was only enough room for Andrzej to squeeze in between the soldiers. I spread my coat on the floor and my leather bag served as a pillow. Just to be in a horizontal position was relief and I fell asleep instantly.

Did someone tug at me? Did someone call my name? Drunk with fatigue, I could not shake myself awake even though I heard Stella scream: "For heaven's sake, Cecylia, wake up!"

Next I felt strong hands griping my arms, someone pulling me to my feet. My eyes opened on the large face of Kuntze.

"Out of here!" he roared. "The barn is on fire. We're being shelled."

I glanced about me in a daze. Everybody had left. The bed was now vacant. There was no one in the kitchen. Then I was outside. In the glow of the flames that were licking the night sky, soldiers were running about. Artillery was roaring, shrapnel was flying. Snow and earth scattered. A sled was hit. The horse bolted away, pulling with it the fireworks of exploding ammunition.

All the while it went on peacefully snowing.

"*Herr* Lieutenant, where is Stella?" I screamed through the din.

"She made a run for it," he shouted back. Then he shouted at his men to get the sleds ready.

There was a deafening roar and suddenly the farm house was on fire. A perfect hit. "My bag!" I screamed. The bag with the electric cooker and the gold coins. But the photograph, my child's photograph . . .

There, in the burning house, I had lost Bruno's photograph and I had lost Stella as well. Stella, my only friend and our child . . .

I shouted into the thunder of fire and explosion, "Steeeeella! Aaaaaaaaaandrzej!" Then I listened for an answer as if it were possible to hear anything. I refused to believe that she had run away. She had encouraged *me* to run away each time we had stopped for the use of a toilet. I told her that either all three of us escape or no one. Was it possible that Stella would not keep her part of the bargain? "Steeeella! Aaaaaaaaandrzej!" I shouted.

At first I could not believe that I actually heard someone responding with my name, so faint was the sound. But I pushed my way through running soldiers in the direction from which that voice seemed to have come.

There she was. There was the child. All three of us hugged

each other, laughing, crying, and laughing once more. I picked up Andrzej, pressed him to my heart and kissed his face. I felt the salty tears on his face, felt the childish body through my heavy coat. I had looked for the child and I had found him!

"Szarek!" It was Kuntze bellowing. "Szarek, on the sled!" he shouted through cupped hands, and for some reason he looked as if he were disappointed that I had found Stella.

My search for the two must have taken place in a circle of a hundred feet, because there was Brucke too. He seemed as furious as Kuntze. He grabbed me, lifted me up — only madness could have given him so much extra energy — and dumped me onto the wet straw. He threw my cane inside. Andrzej and Stella followed.

"Where are our other sleds and the other men?" I asked Brucke.

"What do you think? They left. They didn't want to wait for two stupid women and a spoiled brat. The lieutenant and I and the three of you, that's all. There's just this sled left."

"The Kommandant won't like it but we can't wait for him and the twelve sleds here. When he finds out we'll just have to tell him that the others are unaccounted for."

It was obvious that the men on the seven sleds had deserted. If Kuntze and Brucke had not been so submissive to the Kommandant's orders, they would have deserted too and we would have been free. But they kept an eye on us, probably still believing in their ultimate victory.

While Stella and I made up a nest of straw and blankets for Andrzej, Stella kept talking wildly. "The shelling, and suddenly the barn on fire. I shook you but you wouldn't wake up. I ran out and told Kuntze. He went into the kitchen and carried you out. Shrapnel was flying all around, so I just ran. I didn't know I was running because once in a while I saw Brucke, behind or ahead of me. Then I looked for you. I couldn't see you anywhere. I was out of my mind."

Kuntze swung himself up on the driver's seat, next to Brucke. Cursing, he tried to maneuver the horse through the remaining sleds of the other unit, through scattered crates and debris.

Our progress was hanidcapped by other vehicles also trying to move ahead. After we had gone through the village we found the thoroughfare congested with retreating troops, broken-down cars and wagons. We were open targets for Russian bombers.

The horse suddenly reared as though it had gone berserk, and

I gasped as I glimpsed the sled heading away from the road toward trees. The next moment we were on a silent forest lane. Then we advanced swiftly in the darkness. Later, without any apparent cause, the horse halted, bracing its legs, refused to go any farther.

All except Andrzej got off the sled, but the horse would not budge. I climbed back up to throw off some of the load. Kuntze turned on me, whip in hand. "You bitch, you'll walk like we do. Get down or I'll kill you!" And he struck me. Luckily, my heavy coat protected me from the blow. But Stella, screaming, threw herself at Kuntze and explained what I had wanted to do. He turned his anger on the horse.

Stella followed me up into the sled and pushed down the suitcase containing her few belongings and the bundle of bedding.

How easily she parted with things.

With a twinge I followed her example. I threw off three suitcases. Then she and I took hold of a hamper filled with silverware and let it topple over.

The clatter made Kuntze turn around. He shouted: "I am making you responsible for the destruction of *Ortskommandantur* property." However, he did nothing more. He knew it was the silver or us.

Of all the baggage only my trunk, too heavy for us to lift, and one sack of fodder remained on the sled. The horse was willing now to pull the much lighter load.

It was bitter cold. Kuntze and Brucke on the more exposed driver's seat were beating their backs with their arms.

Ahead we saw the dark humps of a settlement.

41

Kuntze halted at the first hut. It was locked and nobody answered our knocking. We proceeded to the next hut and the next and begged in German and in Polish for shelter. We had to plead with Kuntze to refrain from forcing his way in. He gave in to us. Perhaps he had finally realized that he and Brucke were nothing more than two lonely soldiers on the run.

At last a door opened. A man, his face criss-crossed by a multitude of wrinkles, held up a lantern to look us over. He said his name was Vojtek. He called out to his wife, Valery, and they talked it over. They let us in. They brought straw in from the barn and spread it on the floor of a room in which four children were sleeping in two beds.

We stretched out fully clothed except for Kuntze who moaned as he removed his right boot and sock to bare a dirty foot with a festering wound.

Valery brought him a bucket of water. He was still in the process of soaking and cleaning the wound when he dropped on his side and fell asleep.

Stella and I decided in whispers to wait until we were sure that Brucke was asleep and then we would slip out and ask someone in another house to hide us. But, waiting for the sound of Brucke's snoring, we ourselves fell asleep and, by the time the artillery woke us, it was daylight and both Kuntze and Brucke were already up.

Kuntze could barely walk. "Get ready," he ordered. "We'd better get out of here."

Getting ready only meant pulling our hoods over our heads. We had slept fully dressed.

Not a hundred yards away from Vojtek's home, we saw a burning farm. Then we saw another hut on fire and ahead of us a whole village was one single mass of flames.

Stella touched Lieutenant Kuntze's shoulder and said: "I will not go any farther, even if you shoot me."

"I don't care," Kuntze said. "Get off, lady, and fall into the hands of the Reds." He turned full face from his driver's seat and asked, "What about you, Miss Szarek?" I noticed how weary he looked.

"I'll stay with Stella and the child."

"Is that soooo?"

He stopped the sled. "Get off, man," Kuntze said to Brucke Brucke got off as well. Kuntze took the reins from him, jumped down, held them out to me, and said, "Keep the horse and sled."

"Me?"

He shrugged. "Ach, what the hell. Brucke and I will take to the woods."

"To the woods?" It was the first time I saw Brucke question a superior.

"We'll be less exposed and I bet we'll meet some comrades."

"But your bad foot," I said.

"Get the hell in that driver's seat!"

I hesitated.

Brucke, again the obedient subordinate, was about to push me. I scrambled over.

I had never handled a harnessed horse. Kuntze gave me the whip. I flicked the reins and it began to move. I did not comprehend what was expected of me. "Ho," I said, and the horse stopped. I made it start again, pulling the right rein to get the sled all the way to the side so that there would be enough space for a U turn. I wanted to be as far away as possible from that mass of flames.

Would Kuntze let us go? Or would he, now, put bullets in our backs?

I was too scared to turn my head. Only after there was a distance of two hundred feet between us did I dare to look back.

They were in a white field halfway to the forest. Kuntze, his heavy shoulders sagging, was limping.

"Look at me, Stella," I called over my shoulders. "Can you imagine, the horse obeys me. How about going back to Vojtek's, what do you say?"

"You're the boss."

Vojtek took us in. Valery served us tea and while we got warm we made up a story. "We come from Rodenkov," Stella started out. "It was burned to the ground. We fled and these two Germans took us over and threatened to shoot us if we tried to get away."

"But this morning when we convinced them that we were surrounded and they saw every farm in flames, they took to the woods," I concluded.

"The horse is yours then?" Vojtek asked, shifting his eyes to the window.

"Yes, it's my father's." Then I told him we had no money but we would pay for our keep with clothing from our trunk.

"I'm sure we can come to terms," he said. "I'll take the horse to the stable now."

Through the kitchen window we saw him with the help of a neighbor unload the heavy trunk. He returned holding three hand grenades. "Are these yours?" he asked with a cunning smile on his wrinkled face.

"Good heavens!" Stella exclaimed. "The Germans must have left them."

"I want to report this to the sheriff at once," I said.

"The sheriff is away," Vojtek said. "You don't have to bother, I'll tell him when he comes back. Meanwhile I'll bury them in the yard."

It was still morning. We stretched out on the straw and fell asleep. Valery awakened us for dinner. I was so tired that my eyes kept closing while I was eating. However, I finished everything to the last crumb.

42

"Stella! Stella! Wake up Stella. The Russians are here!"

Stella, rubbing her eyes, mumbled: "Not so loud, Vojtek may hear you."

"Let him hear me. It's over, Stella. We're free."

"That's what you think. If Vojtek sees us so happy, he might suspect we're Jewish," Stella said. "I tell you, I don't trust Vojtek at all. If he should guess we're Jewish he'll have a nice little pogrom all by himself and the whole village will cover for him. He's after that trunk. So, for my sake and his," she glanced at Andrzej, "don't be so excited — no Pole would be."

"Nobody can hear us. We're liberated, Stella! No more hiding, no more lying, no more pretending. Come to the window. Look at them. Their tanks are huge. What a beautiful sight!"

"It's like jumping from the frying pan into the fire. Remember Lvov in 1939?"

"Are you out of your mind? If we shot off our mouths against Stalin, or were caught peddling blackmarket merchandise, then we were in trouble. But so were their own people."

"I don't trust any of them. Communists, Nazis, the lot."

When Stalin and Hitler divided Poland and Lvov fell to the Russians, Jews and Poles alike had resented the invader and, naturally did not appreciate what they called "The Liberation Accomplished Without A Single Shot." As harsh as they were, the Russians did not discriminate particularly against Jews when they were the occupiers of that part of Poland. And after living for almost four years under Nazi occupation I knew the difference and I welcomed the Russians with all my heart.

"I was in Lvov, too," I said. "They arrested my father on suspicion of being involved in the blackmarket, but they were willing to listen to my explanation and let him go. To this day I reproach myself for getting my father out of that Russian prison. Now, they are our liberators, Stella."

"What about the atrocities they committed in Poland? Have you forgotten?"

"The Germans have deported an entire ethnic group. The Russians have arrested and deported people of every ethnic background including their own, but only if they expressed opposition to their kind of socialism. But they permitted people to write to their families and to receive packages. I've never received even a note from my father."

"They're both murderers. If the Germans committed worse crimes, what do you suggest, that they be hanged twice?"

Stella remained on the straw waiting. Her body was tense and on her face there was a hard look. But she could not dampen my excitement.

'Bruno, my Bruno, my little bird almost nine years old! Soon, my son, soon we'll be reunited.' This one thought held me spellbound for the moment.

Through the small panes of the window, I watched the Russian convoy roll by, tank after tank camouflaged with tree branches and brush. Weary looking soldiers in heavy brown coats sat on top of the tanks. The tanks were followed by trucks, command cars, and jeeps.

One jeep pulled up in front of Vojtek's hut and three soldiers came to the door. I felt like running to embrace them. Aware of Stella's warning, I went to the kitchen just to be near them.

They asked Vojtek when the last German had passed through Czuchov and in what direction they had gone. They asked for water for the radiator and when Vojtek went to the pump in the yard to fill the pail, I went to shake hands with my liberators.

They introduced themselves with a bow, copying the Poles, and my heart skipped a beat when I heard that the lieutenant's name was Jakubovicz. It seemed so fantastic that a Jew should casually speak his name that I kept staring at him, transfixed. Had he been a Polish Jew my bright-eyed stare would have tipped him off, but he did not understand, and responded with a wide smile.

The fact that Russian convoys were passing through Czuchov all day long made it clear that we were now behind the front.

I went back and found Stella still resting with Andrzej on the straw. I told her that I intended to start out immediately for Konstancin to see Frania. If she was all right, I would begin the search for Bruno and my parents.

Stella asked Andrzej to play wih his spools of yarn, and to me she said, "I have no place to go. May I go with you?"

"Of course. I figure on five days to reach Konstancin; is it all right with you?"

"It's all right with me."

I asked Vojtek whether he would drive us to Konstancin. The woods were still crawling with Germans, he said, and we would be in danger. No matter what I offered him he refused.

Then, in the evening he took me aside. "Listen, Miss Szarek. My neighbor was about to report you to the Russians because of those hand grenades I found in your sled. I managed to stop him. But if you want to avoid trouble you had better leave first thing in the morning. I tell you what. I'll drive you, but only to Rybnik. That's thirty kilometers from here. You'll be far enough. For pay you give me the horse."

"The horse? How do you suppose we'll get from Rybnik to Konstancin? You know very well that there are no trains or buses."

"Leave the trunk here and come back for it later. Certainly two good-looking girls like you will be offered a lift by someone."

"And stand in the icy road with a small child?"

"He's not your child."

I felt like strangling him. But I had become accustomed to gritting my teeth and keeping quiet. I said: "I've already reported the whole affair to the Russians. They already know about the grenades." It was only one more lie added to the countless falsehoods that circumstances had forced me to employ. "They told me that they could not be bothered with such a small matter at this time. Once the administration is reorganized, they'll put the affair on file. As for our means of transport we'll do just fine on our own."

As Vojtek had his eye on both the horse and the trunk he was sure to use any treachery to get them. Stella thought that he might even knife us in our sleep.

We took turns standing guard.

Next morning through the window in our room I saw Vojtek leaving the yard with the hand grenades. I ran out, caught up with him, and faced him.

"I'm afraid to keep them," he stammered. "You see, if the Russians found them they would blame *me*, so I'm taking them to the Russians."

"You want me to get in trouble."

"All I want is the horse, Miss Szarek. You give me the horse and I'll bury the grenades."

"Blackmailing us, are you? Take it from me, you won't get the horse!"

With me at his heels, he made a beeline for a group of soldiers milling around. To my relief I saw among them Jakubovicz, and before Vojtek could open his mouth, I said in my broken Russian: "Officer, these grenades belonged to some Germans who confiscated my horse and sled and kept me and my girlfriend as hostages. It was only after we had managed to get away from them that we found their grenades on our sled." Did he understand my Russian?

Jakubovicz calmly reached for one of the grenades still in Vojtek's hands, pulled the fuse, and hurled it into the woods toward the same spot where Kuntze and Brucke had disappeared thirty hours befoe. With the detonation, five Russians tossed their caps into the air and yelled joyfully. Jakubovicz offered the second grenade to a comrade and his throw was celebrated in the same fashion. I realized that they thought they had killed some Germans hiding in the woods. Open-mouthed, Vojtek watched the three hand grenades explode. Jakubovicz dusted his hands and said, "*Charaszo* (O.K.)?"

I nodded gratefully. But I knew the sooner Stella and I left Vojtek's house the better.

Upon my return to the hut, Stella told me that she had found a young Pole who would gladly be our driver. He was one of the stragglers the Germans had picked off the street in Warsaw and put in a road-gang.

Kazik was a stocky man in his twenties. His plain-featured face with a reddish mustache struck me as friendly enough. After a handshake that symbolized our agreement all four of us went to the stable.

The horse was gone.

We stood dumbfounded. "*Psia krew* (Bloody dog)!" Kazik cursed, and ran back to the hut.

When I burst into the kitchen, Kazik had Vojtek by the throat. "Son of a bitch, I'll kill you," he shouted.

Valery was screaming. Kazik loosened his grip just enough to allow Vojtek to tell him where the horse was. His voice rasping, he admitted that he had given it to a Russian and offered to show us the way to a farm house outside the village where several companies had set up camp.

"If you try any tricks," Kazik said, "I'll keep my promise, I'll kill you."

Only I went into the house Vojtek pointed out to me. Kazik stayed with him outside.

I asked for the officer in charge and hoped it would be Jakubovicz. Disappointed to see a stranger I said: "The man outside stole my horse, and now one of your soldiers has got it."

"My soldiers wouldn't take anything from the Polish people." He glanced out the window. "That old man? Sure. He was here earlier. He gave his horse to Vasil as a way of saying 'thank you' for being liberated."

"He had no right to give it away. It's mine."

"Vasil," the officer addressed a stubby soldier who was brewing something on the stove. "That horse you got belongs to this woman. Give it back."

"My own horse limps, comrade," Vasil said. "You wouldn't like me to chase the Germans on a lame horse."

"Then give her yours."

Vasil mumbled something and asked me to follow him to the stable. "Wait outside," he said. It took at least five minutes before he came out with a horse so minute I could put my arm around his neck without raising my arm.

Vasil stroked the shaggy brown rump. "Sybirek, old friend, this is your new mistress." When he turned to me, his eyes were wet. "He's a fine horse," he said to me. "He's been with me all the way from my village near Odessa. Be kind to him. He likes sugar." Touching the horse's muzzle, he said: "*Do swidania* (See you soon) . . ." and abruptly left.

I stroked the small lame animal. "I'll see you get well, Sybirek," I said, and led him out of the yard.

Both Vojtek and Kazik broke out laughing when they saw Sybirek. "What do you have there?" Kazik asked.

"They gave me this in exchange for my horse."

Vojtek laughed. "My dog Rex is bigger."

"Better than nothing —" I said meekly.

"Let's see if he can make it to the other side of the road," Kazik teased. "Miss Szarek is sorry for him because he limps like she does.

I stared at Kazik and Vojtek. Enemies a short while back, they had now become united in their ridicule of pathetic little Sybirek. "Come," I patted the horse's head.

Not until I was inside Vojtek's stable did I really look him over. Though he limped, he had strong legs. The slanted eyes peering through the long mane were as sad as the eyes of his former master.

"Never mind them, Sybirek. You made it from Russia to Poland. You'll make it from Czuchov to Konstancin."

In response Sybirek neighed.

The following day Kazik harnessed Sybirek to the big sled. To encourage him I held out a lump of sugar. He nipped at my fingers as if to express his gratitude.

I climbed into the front seat beside Kazik, took the whip from his hand, and gave it to Andrzej who was in the back with his mother. Then we were off to Konstancin.

Vojtek's dog, whom his owner thought was as big as Sybirek, ran after us barking. He tried to jump on the sled and Andrzej who had grown fond of him began to cry, while I shouted: "Go home, Rex, go home."

The dog stopped barking and the next time I looked back, he was gone.

43

Although he was lame, Sybirek trotted steadily on. Once in a while the stillness of the empty road through the woods was shattered by distant shots. The sight of two corpses in German uniform laying by the roadside gave me a feeling of satisfaction. Then, when I saw more and more of them, my pleasure began to ebb. How pitiful they looked, like discarded puppets. "How small they are," I said.

"They shrink in the cold," Kazik said. There was no pity in him.

After two hours on the road, a column of Russian soldiers approached from the opposite direction. We prepared to show our identity papers, but they neither stopped us nor did they ask any questions.

Sybirek began to limp more severely so the three adults got off the sled and walked alongside or behind it. Each of us took turns to rest on the sled. When my turn came, I sat near Andrzej and covered my feet with his blanket. I felt something soft and warm moving. It was Rex!

"Andrzej!" I exploded.

The child burst into tears.

He was Bruno crying.

Bruno had brought home a black mongrel and begged to be allowed to keep him. Mark said the dog was probably diseased, but gave in. He warned the child that if he did not behave, the dog would have to go.

Bruno no longer made a fuss about going to bed at eight, brushing his teeth, or eating his spinach, but put up with everything out of love for Blacky. One day, however, the dog disappeared. I finally traced him to one of my neighbors. She told me that Bruno had turned up on her doorstep with the dog, and confessed to having broken his father's pipe stand. Feeling certain that his pet would now be sent away, he had wanted at least to make sure that he had a good home, so, remembering that she had often given him cookies, he had hoped she also might be good to his dog. In his handkerchief he had had some scraps of meat saved over from dinner, and he had promised to bring more food so that Blacky would be no burden to her.

I had the pipe stand repaired without Mark's or Bruno's knowledge. When I told Bruno that the pipe stand was all right he leapt into my arms, his round eyes shining, and then ran to get his dog back.

Hugging Andrzej, I said: "Don't cry, so we have another passenger . . .

"Thank you Pani (Miss) Cecylia, thank you." Throwing his arm around the dog, he looked up at me and said: "Is the dog mine now?"

"I guess so. He chose you instead of Vojtek, didn't he?"

We decided to stop for lunch near a clump of trees which protected us from the wind. I asked Kazik to measure out a good portion of oats and when Sybirek stuck his head into the fodder bag, I stroked his neck.

Stella handed each of us a pork chop between two slices of bread that she had ordered in Czuchov, and the bottle filled with tea made the rounds. This was a feast even though the tea was cold.

When half an hour later Andrzej complained that he was hungry we were puzzled. But that evening at dinner we caught him feeding his portion to Rex.

"None of that, you little brat," Kazik raged. "You damn well eat your food. I won't do with less because you give your portion to the dog.

When the supplies we had with us were finished, we tried to buy something in the villages through which we passed but everywhere we were told they had nothing to spare. I still had a diamond hidden in my lipstick which I kept in my coat pocket but I was afraid to take it out since in that kind of confusion it could easily have become a motive for murder.

I started to measure out smaller rations for Sybirek.

Lame and with a sore on his side from the rubbing of the harness, hungry and often thirsty, dragging a load too heavy for him, gallant little Sybirek still kept going.

At the next village I took a woolen dress from the trunk and tried to exchange it for food, but in the end I had to return to the sled and tell Stella, "No deal."

"I'll try," Stella said. She lifted Andrzej off the sled and, without the woolen dress, walked away with him. While I waited for her I saw her in my mind timidly knocking at a door and, her face flushed, begging for a piece of bread for her child.

It started to snow. The wind blew Sybirek's mane in all directions. I asked Kazik to cover the horse with his blanket but sarcastically he replied: "Let the fancy lady do it herself. I've had enough. Why should I put up with that damn kid and that stupid dog and nothing to eat? Why should I run around to find a pump and draw water and 'Kazik do this and Kazik do that!' I'll be quitting soon."

"Quit right now," I said sharply.

"I'll quit in my own good time," he retorted.

"Cover the horse!" I ordered.

Mumbling under his mustache, Kazik climbed off the sled and flung the blanket over Sybirek's rump.

"Fasten it so that it won't blow off."

He did as he was told.

The cold cut into my lungs like a knife, and now with every breath I felt pain. It will pass, I told myself, and pulled the blanket up over my mouth.

Finally I saw Stella and Andrzej emerge from the whirling snow. When they were close enough, I reached for the child, brushed the snow off his shoulders and cap, and quickly wrapped him in a blanket. Stella emptied her coat pockets: five slices of dark bread, each of a different size and thickness; a small jar holding one ounce of oil; one hard-boiled egg; two onions; four raw potatoes and one slice of white bread.

Andrzej grabbed the white bread, took one bite, and stuffed the rest into the dog's mouth.

"I'll throttle that damn dog," Kazik exploded.

Rex, fangs bared, snarled at him.

Andrzej started to cry.

We agreed that Andrzej would get the entire egg and all he could eat. When he had finished, Stella divided what remained into three equal parts. The raw potatoes she would cook later wherever we stopped for the night.

I took Stella's hand between mine to somehow let her know that I was aware of what an ordeal begging must have been to her. The next day and the following, she went to beg, again and again.

During the next four days skirts and blouses as well as yard goods and sheets passed from my trunk into the linen chest of a miller's wife. We ate in her house; we washed; we slept in beds. When the miller's wife had taken all she wanted she sent us away. Nonetheless, the four days of rest in a warm house and eating cooked food had restored our strength. Our fairly successful battle against body lice as well as the sight of Kazik's departure had improved our morale. And, to crown it all, I was able to barter the rejected woolen dress for four pounds of sugar.

Sybirek was rested and the wound on his side had healed. When I put on the large harness I wondered how long it would be until it rubbed the sore open again. The miller, who looked on, advised us to take the horse to a blacksmith.

The blacksmith found a splinter lodged in Sybirek's hoof and removed it.

From my blouse I pulled out a bracelet of gold which I had bought after the robbery as a substitute for those Glasseye had taken from me. I put it into the blacksmith's hand. Without a word he produced a smaller harness that fitted Sybirek.

Freed of the splinter, freshly shod and properly harnessed, Sybirek trotted off neighing, swishing his tail, and shaking his mane. He did not mind now pulling the sled with all three of us on it and, as if fate had taken a turn for the better in every way, the farther we advanced toward Warsaw, the more hospitable and generous people became.

Relieved of the German oppressor their hearts seemed to have opened to those who tried to make their way home.

Stella and I talked endlessly. We talked about our past and we talked about our hopes and we talked about our plans for the future. Stella described how her husband had been shot in Lvov in front of their house. She told me that she had promised him to emigrate with Andrzej.

"Where will you go?" I asked her.

"To Palestine. And you?"

"First I have to see if Frania is alive. Then I'll go to Zloczov and Niemirov and then I'll take Bruno to America."

"Do you have relatives there?"

"No."

"Why America?"

"Because of Lincoln."

"Lincoln?"

"He was the president of the United States many years ago. From being a lumberjack and poor, too poor to go to school (all he knew was self-taught) the Americans voted him to the highest office. They realized he was a very exceptional man and did not mind his shoddy clothes, his odd appearance, or his awkward ways. America will make Bruno the kind of man I want him to be."

"You don't speak their language. How will you make a living there?"

"I'll learn their language. All who have gone there before me have learned it. None came back."

The closer we got to Warsaw the more crowded the road became. Finally it was a solid flowing mass of people on foot, sleds, wagons, and bicycles; a stream of pilgrims for a holy shrine.

Questions were shouted from vehicle to vehicle:

"Where are you from?"

"Where did they drag you?"

"On what street were you living in Warsaw?"

"Is it true they burned every single building?"

I added my own questions: "Have you come across a family named Gorski? A girl by the name of Maria Lasocka? No? Perhaps you have met Zosia Szarbecka? And, to a gray-haired Polish man walking on the side of the road, I called, "Where are you going?"

"To Warsaw, *Madamé.*"

"But I thought that Poles were not allowed access to Warsaw."

"Not anymore. The ban was lifted as soon as the Germans left," he answered in an educated voice.

I turned to Stella. "We'll go via Warsaw." And I then invited the gray-haired gentleman to join us on the sled.

He stepped up beside me, took the reins from my hands, and said: "*Madame,* allow me."

How good it felt to have my callused hands relieved!

He clicked his tongue and Sybirek galloped off.

"My name is Lucien Skovron," he said, bowing to me and Stella.

"I can see that you know how to handle horses."

"I do, and a very nice little horse you have here." He could not have said anything that pleased me more.

At the outskirts of Warsaw Sybirek tried to pull us over mounds of rubble and debris. All of us got off to help him, pushing the sled over the worst spots.

"I'm afraid the going will become worse." He paused, then said, "I have a villa not far from here. How about going there and seeing whether there is anything of it left."

Optimist, I thought. But since it would soon be night, Stella and I agreed. We left the main road and walked beside the sled, alongside the fences of snow-covered gardens. Most of the villas had been burned. Some had been spared, but they were still deserted.

"It doesn't look so good," Skovron said. "Shall we continue, or shall we take over one of those deserted houses?"

"Even if only your cellar is still intact, I'd prefer to take shelter on your property," I said.

We continued in silence, tired and in suspense.

Suddenly Skovron stopped walking and in a jubilant tone of voice cried out: "Jesus, there it is, Miss Szarek! My house! It's still there!"

The stucco was riddled with bullet holes, a piece of roof was gone, window-panes were shattered, and the entrance door was swinging in the wind. Yet, Skovron laughed with joy. He fell to his knees, crossed himself, got up, motioned toward the door with a bow and, like a duke offering the hospitality of his castle, he said, "Welcome."

In the windy house we found many books, a piano, a French provincial desk, and a couple of chairs. Skovron went from room to room listing aloud the oriental rugs, the beds, chairs, lamps, and other things that had disappeared. But even these losses did not diminish his happiness.

The large country-size kitchen in the back of the house was undamaged, and some windows had panes. Stella reached into the woodbox and started a fire in the stove. Skovron unharnessed Sybirek and such was his affection for my midget that he led him through the entrance hall and the living room into what must have been a maid's room. He unearthed some burlap sacks which he nailed across the open windowframe.

To improvise beds for us, he took doors off their hinges and suspended them across chairs and stools. Burlap sacks and our coats were our bedding, an improvement to sleeping on straw spread on floors.

In the meantime, Stella had put the few potatoes she had collected on the stove and Skovron had placed some pickles he had found in the cellar on the table. A real feast. Fate had been good to us.

First thing in the morning, while Stella and Skovron were on a forage hunt for potatoes, cabbage, preserves, and even canned food, in the cellars of neighboring houses, I went to Warsaw.

44

The destruction of the city had been complete. Here and there a wall was still standing, its smoke-blackened window-holes looking like empty eyesockets. Chimneys that had withstood the destruction stretched heavenward like the arms of gigantic corpses.

With the help of my cane I climbed the heaps of debris and sandbag barricades. Now and then I had to find my way around overturned tramways. The only undamaged buildings were the headquarters of the Special Commandos who directed the systematic burning of the city.

Beyond at the Three Crosses Square where Rolf had been shot, the facade of a five-story building had been ripped away and I could look into the rooms as though a stage-curtain had been raised. The nursery, with its flowery wallpaper, crib, and white chest with a teddybear on it, gave me the illusion that a mother, formula-bottle in hand, would enter at any moment.

There was no sign of the photography shop where Rolf made his last errand before he was murdered.

People were foraging in the debris, picking out a saucepan, a board, a nail, a soggy blanket. A piece of yellow cardboard attached to a broomstick announced in handwritten lettering that there was a restaurant where one could get soup, hot tea, and bread. I gathered up whatever strength I had and climbed up the mountain of rubble towards it.

In a tent, the young proprietress welcomed me. Her equipment was a primus-stove and a large steaming pot. My mouth watered in anticipation of a hot plate of soup and a piece of bread. After having lost the cooker containing the gold coins, I could offer only some wearing apparel from the trunk in exchange for food. I still did not dare to take the diamond out of the lipstick. What could I give her in exchange for a meal? I sat down to think. Than I had a brainstorm. I offered the proprietress my leather gloves. She was happy to serve me.

Revived, I set out for the railroad station which now, according to the proprietress had become the center of the capital. "People come here first form all over and then they go to their homes to see whether they can find some of their belongings. For those already living in the city it has become a meeting place. It's not far from here," she said, and showed me a short cut.

On remnants of walls and the sides of some intact train-cars pieces of paper were pasted and empty match boxes had names scribbled on them in pen, pencil, or lipstick telling that so and so was alive, had been there, and could be reached at a given address.

It took me two hours to scrutinize every paper, every matchbox, to no avail. I found no one I knew.

Many people were moving around me. Some had stopped and were reading, like myself, over the shoulders of others. I lingered among them. Suddenly my heart skipped a beat.

There was Zosia!

It was undoubtedly her. She was wearing a pair of man's trousers, a brown mackinow jacket, a man's soft felt hat — which was apparently what Warsaw's women were wearing these days. I called out to her and she let out a joyful shout. The next moment we were in each other's arms. Finally Zosia said, "Let's get out of here and go to my house."

"It's still standing?"

She smiled a mischievious smile. "You'll see," she said.

I would not have recognized Szopena Street nor Zosia's house. Like all the other buildings, it was a heap of rubble, the heap leaned against the corner of two outside walls which were still standing and rose high above the debris.

Unperturbed, Zosia led the way up. The going was tricky because snow covered the loose bricks. "I've built the stairplanks myself, but the thawing snow and the rain keep loosening them."

Only now did I perceive that there were steps underfoot.

"Give me your hand," Zosia said. "The last bit is steep." And she pulled me up to the top of the rubble heap from where we looked down into the street as if from a large terrace. Behind us, nestled into the corner of two walls, was a shack. It was incongruous to see Zosia put a key into the door. It seemed as if a single kick would have brought down the entire structure. When she opened the door she had to hold it so that it would not fall from its hinges. Bowing ceremoniously, as had Skovron, she invited me in.

A king-size brass bed took up almost all of the available space. Brightly colored Persian rugs covered the walls and the floor. Two wicker chairs stood on either side of a wooden crate that was covered with an embroidered Madeira tablecloth. The ceiling was constructed of scavenged doors.

The room reminded me of a child's secret hideout. It was enchanting. "I don't remember this bed and these rugs," I said.

"Of course not. Our belongings are buried under here," she pointed to the floor. "Who knows when we'll be able to dig them up. But, like everybody else, we went on *szaber* expeditions."

"*Szaber?*"

"Loot," she said. "So far, Vaclava and I have managed pretty well . . ."

"You and Vaclava are together?"

"We teamed up to survive. People in Warsaw live in groups now."

"I'm dying to see her," I cried, overjoyed to hear that Vaclava was alive. With Vaclava I could talk about Rolf more openly.

"Right now she's out hunting for food."

"Did she hear anything from her brother?"

"Not a word."

I could see blue sky through the broken doors that had been made into a ceiling. "What if it rains?" I asked.

"We sleep under umbrellas and dry our bedding outside after the rain stops." She smiled at me. "Why don't you move in with us? That bed is big enough for three."

"Thank you, Zosia, but first I have a few things to look after. It will take at least a few weeks. Then, if you still want me I might take you up on your offer." I was tired and went to sit down.

"Not on the chairs," Zosia cried. "Vaclava has to fix them. She's the handyman in this household. Sit on the bed." She pushed the featherquilts to the wall and I sank down against them.

Over a glass of tea from a thermos she told me of the evacuation from Warsaw to the Pruszkov Transition Camp; then to the village of Skiernice; she told me of her work on a farm; her fun in learning how to milk a cow. Then she told me about Maria.

Maria had received word from her brother — whom Rolf had once managed to get out of prison where he had been sent by the Germans on the charge of violation of some postal regulation — that now he had been detained by the Polish underground for giving the Germans secret signs that pointed out the weak spots in the city's defense system.

Maria had assumed that the confession that her brother was a Jew would automatically clear him. She was wrong. The Polish underground searched her, found one thousand American dollars on her, and detained her as well as her brother.

Zosia, who vouched for Maria's Polish patriotism, was threatened with arrest if she didn't mind her own business.

Maria Losocka and her brother were shot as German spies.

Maria had saved a thousand dollars from her job in Vinetta so that she could buy a second-hand piano and some pretty clothes once the war ended and "Storm the world." Instead, her careful savings had brought about her death. And I had had some part in it.

One day before the uprising, she had made one of her wry remarks: "If the war lasts a bit longer I'll reach my goal."

Her aim was to have exactly a thousand American dollars. She was short of fifty-two.

On an impulse, I gave her fifty-two. Then I said, "Now there was nothing to prevent the war from ending."

In one of her rare emotional outbursts, she threw her arms around me and both of us laughed happily. The uprising against the Germans was about to take place and we believed that the Polish government in exile was going to arrive from England at any moment. Best of all, both of us were alive. There was reason to laugh and to be generous.

But instead of wearing pretty clothes and "storming the world," Maria was dead. For once in her life she had been willing to do something for someone else, and she was dead.

In a way I envied her.

"Zosia,. do you believe Maria's brother was a spy?"

"Are you mad? He was Jewish, but not a spy. One would have to exclude the other. It's money that did it. And I believe it wasn't the underground but that, in the terrible confusion, some gangsters took over. It was impossible for me to establish who they were. but you wait till I find that bastard interrogator!"

The following morning, against Stella's objections that my cold was getting worse, I went to Warsaw once more. I read the names on papers pasted on the crumbling walls and searched the faces of people in the streets.

"Who are those skeletons in striped pajamas?" I asked the restaurant proprietress who was busy cooking *bigos* (a Polish dish, a concoction of pickled cabbage, cabbage, dry mushrooms, bones, meats, vegetables and leftovers) on her primus.

"Jewish survivors from the Death Camps."

I ran toward two of these living ghosts. "Have you seen Lejzor Brand?" I asked. And then I wondered at myself. In my wildest dreams I could not have separated my father from his garb of a Hassid and connected him with skeletons in such a getup.

Their heads shook from side to side.

Three other Death Camp survivors shuffled by. I asked: "Do you by any chance know a Lejzor Brand? — a lawyer Rathauser? a Julius Fischer? — a Hersh Halbertal?"

Hollow eyes stared at me. A death's head shook from left to right.

I was not sure he understood.

I asked others. I asked and asked and asked.

But it was not until I invited one of them for a bowl of soup that I began to grasp the truth. I was told by an eyewitness what had taken place in Majdanek, Treblinka, Auschwitz and Dachau. Now I realized that all the terrible information in the underground news-sheets and all the incredible grapevine rumors were true. Now, Maria's macabre joke concerning Kovalski's transformation into lavender soap struck me with all its horror.

"All are gone, all are gone . . ." the survivor said, as he finished a little chunk of meat from the soup.

My father too? Perele, Fischer, Mark?

But there were some suvivors; perhaps my father at this very moment was on some street here in Warsaw searching for me.

And my child —?

My eyes raked the face of every child. I checked the color of hair, the gait, the expression. I stopped many of them, frightening them with my questions. I asked one skinny little lad, "Are you sure you were not called Bruno way back when you were little?"

My look-out post was outside a rummage store, at the busiest corner near the railroad station. The store owner, an elderly woman, came out to chase me away because she said, I was obstructing her window display. In tears I tried to make her understand why I could not leave my post. She shrugged, and let me remain.

A little boy went by muttering: "Two boxes of matches — two boxes of matches —"

"What's your name?" I asked. "Is it Bruno?"

He stared at me.

"Do you have a mole on your left shoulder?"

He bolted away.

I slumped down onto the curbstone. Feeling absolutely exhausted, I began to cry.

The store owner helped me up and into the store. "You have a fever," she said. She poured me a glass of tea, gave me a lump of sugar, and asked: "Where in Warsaw did you leave the boy?"

I left him in Zloczov . . . With a Polish family . . ."

"Zloczov?" She gave me a peculiar glance. "Go home, my dear, go home. Your child is all right . . . Don't cry, he's all right I assure you."

45

That night I couldn't stop coughing.

When Stella saw me in the morning, she said I looked feverish and should leave for Konstancin at once where I might find a doctor. I knew she was right but I was afraid of facing one more loss. No matter what I thought of, the question was always there: Had Frania survived the German retreat and the Russian onslaught? I told Stella that I had to postpone going to Konstancin because I had to visit Rolf's grave before leaving Warsaw.

The German cemetery, I found, was now guarded by Russians, and I did not dare to admit that I had come to visit the grave of a German.

I pretended to have lost my way. They directed me to the entrance of the Polish cemetery and, as their eyes were following me, I had to go where they directed.

I attached myself to a group of mourners around a freshly dug grave.

And there, at a stranger's funeral, I mourned my love.

46

Coughing spells wracked me on my way from the cemetery. I turned hot and cold and obviously had a fever. I wondered whether I would have enough stamina to get to Skovron's villa.

The driver helped me to the entrance door. Stella, without saying a word, led me to a chair by the stove. She pulled my boots off and dried my feet with a burlap rag. Then, handing me a glass of vodka, she said, "Drink it all at once."

"Frania, I need you," I said.

"I am not Frania, I am Stella." I heard her scared voice as if from a great distance. "Just stay where you are, Cecylia, until we're ready to leave. You'll be in Konstancin tonight. I promise."

I was vaguely aware of her running in and out, calling Skovron, calling Andrzej, calling Rex.

The next thing I knew, I was on the sled lying on the straw. Skovron was in the driver's seat. Or was it Kuntze? "Lieutenant, please, not so fast, we'll hit the tree!"

Did moments or hours pass after which I felt Stella pulling me up? To understand what she wanted of me required more effort than I could muster.

"Cecylia dear, look, is this the house?"

"The house . . ." I took off the mitten, rubbed my eyes, and the first thing I saw was Antony's gatehouse and Frania's face behind the window.

"Dear God, let it not be a dream," I prayed.

I scrambled off the sled. When my feet hit the ground, Frania was there, and she and I were locked in an embrace.

47

It was a few weeks later that a Jewish survivor from Zloczov told me that Mark and Bruno and Mark's family had been among the first to be deported.

I went from one end of the country to the other but could find no trace of them.

I had recovered from pneumonia, had finally thrown away the cane, and now was working for the Agricultural Department under the Ministry of Industry headed by Minister Minc.

At my own request I was included in a delegation departing for Stettin. Our mission: to take stock of German businesses and factories that had been reclaimed by the Polish government.

The delegation, consisting of three men and myself, was equipped with credentials which opened all doors. We were put up at the best hotel in Stettin and we were armed with guns for our own protection.

It was for the sake of this last that I had volunteered for the mission.

Only six weeks after the German retreat, Stettin was still in total chaos.

In contrast to the orderly manner in which the Russian Army had triumphantly crossed the territory populated by Poles and Ukrainians, in Stettin (a city populated by Germans), they roamed the streets, molesting German nationals and doing whatever they liked. Violence was commonplace. I remembered their disciplined behavior when they had liberated Czuchov, how they had rescued me from Vojtek's clutches. It was hard for me to believe that these same men looted, raped, and murdered people in Stettin. Corpses were found on streets and in apartments and, after some preliminary inquiries by the Temporary City Administration, no investigation followed.

Fifty Germans were assigned to us daily to do work connected with inventory-taking. They received minimum wages and had no protection.

At last I saw the possibility of realizing my pledge to kill eight Germans.

Though my three co-workers had far less reason to hate the Germans than myself, they had experienced enough hardship not to protest when acts of vengeance were perpetrated. And I was still Cecylia Szarek, a Pole, one of their own. I would be running no risk with them, even if they caught me in the act.

I made one plan after another as to how to go about it, but none of them were feasible.

One morning a young German woman, who had been assigned to us, arrived with her seven-year-old daughter saying she had no one with whom to leave the child. She asked to be excused but was refused.

The little girl's hair was plaited in two dirty braids. From time to time she picked up the hem of her dress to wipe her running nose. The facts were proving very different, I thought, from the supposed fanatical cleanliness of the Germans. All at once the beginning of a feeling of compassion for the child was replaced by a wave of revulsion.

"*Sei brav* (be good) Anni," said her mother, and she went upstairs.

Anni started to run here and there about the large warehouse. She climbed crates, raced down the stairs to the basement, opened doors to offices and slammed them shut, laughing and squealing as though she were in a playground. She was scolded more than once, but that didn't stop her.

Many of the agricultural machines were stored in the basement which was divided into corridors like tunnels. At some point I became aware of the fact that Anni had been down for a long time.

The shadow of an idea began to germinate in a dark corner of my mind but I banished it and went back to work. The shadow reappeared. The child would be a start.

I began to think about it.

Her child for my child. Her pain for mine. I had come to a decision.

My heart hammering, I walked slowly down the stairs to the basement. It took some time for my eyes to grow accustomed to the dim light that came from a single unshaded bulb hanging from the ceiling.

"Anni," I called, and the echo told me my voice had trembled.

Anni appeared, disappeared. Then I heard her giggling senselessly.

"Anni, come here!" My thin shrill voice, the words repeated by the hollow echo, must have frightened her, for she stopped and came out from behind a large crate and stood facing me with a solemn expression.

"I told you to come here! Here!" I pointed at the cement floor directly in front of me.

Anni took a number of slow steps in my direction and came to a halt about ten feet away, next to the front of a mowing machine.

"Have you any brothers or sisters?" I asked.

"No."

"Where is your father?"

"I don't know."

"Anni, stop picking your nose!"

I could not have selected a more appropriate victim.

My voice, trembling no longer, became that of the officer ordering Bruno to strip before he was gassed.

I watched my pale tender-skinned child, his round blue eyes bewildered as he obeyed the Nazi command. I saw him naked now and saw him quickly cover the mole on his left shoulder. And that is when my hand dug inside my pocketbook and took hold of the gun. A shudder went through my body. My fingers tightened over the cold metal and I heard my father say: 'You promised to build a temple to my memory. Is this the cornerstone?'

"Father, this is for you too," I answered. But why was he looking at me in that forbidding manner? Why was he beginning to turn his back? "Father, I'm doing it for your Perele and for your only son, and for his little Lisa, and for your two daughters. I tell you what, I'll kill only this one, Father. Only this one. I promise."

I felt the safety-catch against my palm.

"Anni, for God's sake, stand still!" I screamed.

But she hadn't moved. She stood like a stone staring at me with her large blue eyes.

"Anni, stand still, you dirty brat. No — come here you vermin, you. Come here!"

The child took two more steps forward. Now she was a perfect target.

When I heard the click of the barrel, now ready to shoot, I began to insult her mother, her father, her murderous countrymen. "Come here," I screamed at the top of my lungs.

Suddenly she hurried and stopped directly in front of me, whimpering over and over, "*Mutti* (Mami), I want *Mutti* . . ."

"Shut up, you beast! That's what you are, a beast, born and bred by beasts."

Unaccountably my fingers had loosened their hold on the gun. I tried to tighten them but the gun slipped from their slack wet grip to the bottom of my pocketbook. My hand fell onto the glossy wrapper of a chocolate candy bar. With a will of its own, it snatched up the bar, drew it out and flung it at Anni.

She jumped to catch it, with a grimy little paw. Then she bolted past me and started ruuning up the stairs. She was howling.

I had to admit, finally, that I was incapable of carrying out my pledge. Knowing that, nothing any longer stood in the way to emigrate.

48

"T he Americans call this kind of weather 'Indian summer,' " a fellow-immigrant said in Polish as we stood in line on deck of the 'Ernie Pyle,' before the desk of the United States Immigration Authorities, just outside the port of New York.

Since I had been born in Vienna I had come in under the Austrian quota. That was why, when my turn came and one of the officials faced me, he interrogated me in German.

He asked me so many questions that I soon realized something was wrong. Then I understood him to imply that I was a German trying illegally to steal into the country.

I started to talk Yiddish to a representative of the American Joint Distribution Committee and listed some Jewish holidays but I still did not get that important tag that everybody before me had already pinned to their shirts.

If it had not been so serious, I would have laughed. My situation was bizarre, to say the least.

With my handkerchief I dabbed the drops of perspiration from my face and thought hard of the kind of arguments I could use to prove I was a Jew.

One word came to my mind, which had rescued twenty-one Jews from deportation in the Warsaw Ghetto.

"A *vade* (of course)," I said in that special intonation, while looking directly at the representative of the Joint Distribution Committee. Smiling, he winked back at me by closing one eye for a split second. Then he turned to the immigration officer and said something in English which I did not understand. Finally I got my tag, I pinned it quickly to my blouse, picked up my suitcase and walked toward the exit. There I stopped short, unable to make myself leave the ship. I sat down on my suitcase. Newcomers were being welcomed by relatives or friends. I heard names called and I saw joyful embraces. I had nobody here.

I had no money.

I spoke not a word of English.

I was scared.

Through my tear-filled eyes I saw the same young man from the Joint approaching me. I looked up at him as he said in Yiddish: "What's your name again?"

"My real name or my assumed name?"

"Don't be afraid. Your real name, of course!"

I took a deep breath. "Roma Brand," I said. It was the first time after years of lying that I spoke *my* name clearly and loudly.

"All right, Roma," the man said. "Why don't you go ashore?"

"I don't know where to go, I have no one here."

He smiled at me. "You have all of us," he said softly. Then he reached out for my hand and pulled me up.

Keeping hold of me, he picked up the suitcase with his other hand and led me to the gangplank. Alongside this young man I stepped onto American soil.

EPILOGUE

For me, my child has remained alive. He is with me whenever I want him. Just closing my eyes for a moment brings him back, tugging at my skirt, asking me the endless questions he used to ask years ago.

Sometimes I see him riding his bicycle, sometimes he is climbing onto Sybirek's back. Sybirek trots along and Bruno, with shining blue eyes and wild cries, encourages him to gallop faster and faster. He bends the upper part of his body and presses his pale face in Sybirek's flowing mane. At other times he splashes the water in his tin bathtub and, seeing me watching and smiling at him, he rubs his nose against mine. Then there are times that he curls up with me in my bed, and I let him stay as long as he wants to. I never scold Bruno now. those days are over.

"Bruno, you are the only child I have ever had," I murmur fiercely to a little boy that only I can see. "Nothing can come between us any more!"

THE RIGHTEOUS GENTILES

THE RIGHTEOUS GENTILES

During the three years of my masquerade in Warsaw, I had to be constantly alert because the danger of being discovered lurked at all times. I have been living now as a free person in America for over fifty years, and I still have difficulties falling asleep at night. Many nights I cannot sleep at all. And since gas showers meant extermination, I cannot take a shower. I soak in a bathtub instead. And because I was forced to lie for three years, I cannot lie. Even a little white lie. I just cannot lie.

Ten days after my arrival in New York on September 21, 1947, I found a simple job that didn't require knowledge of English. I painted brightly-colored designs on silk blouses and ties, which were fashionable at that time. The $45 a week I received for my work made me feel independent. It covered food, a furnished room, a dress from a discount store, and even a shipment of coal to my newly-wed sister and her husband, still in Vienna. The complicated procedure of bringing them to the United States took me a year. My sister is now a mother of three children and has eight grandchildren. My bloodline has survived.

Fate has been kind to me.

In 1951 I got married after my husband-to-be agreed to my condition not to have children. I wanted to keep my little son in my heart without competition for my affection. I kept my vow to the extent of enduring two abortions. I have never regretted my decision.

Now I close my eyes and see my son's round blue eyes fixed on me. I hear his voice. "Mamusiu (Mommy), when I grow up I want to be a dentist."

"Why a dentist?" I ask, surprised.

"I heard grandma say to Blume, 'You are in such pain, go to the dentist, he will help you.' I want to help too."

These words ring in my ears whenever I see someone in need. My son, if he had been allowed to grow up, would have found a way to help.

Perhaps this is his legacy.

I hear his childish but resolute voice again. "I want to help!"

My son is not gone.

I have had three books published. *I Dared to Live* has been translated and is available in four countries. In Israel it was a best seller. A docudrama adapted from *I Dared to Live* was shown a few times on television in Poland.

As a volunteer speaker for the Simon Wiesenthal Center, I have been assigned to speak to many diverse audiences—for the last four years mostly to Catholic and Afro-American high schools and colleges. These assignments give me the opportunity to talk about my sweet little boy, about my virtuous father, both good people, both killed in the gas chambers in Belzec.

I talk about my sister's survival and my own, thanks to another virtuous man, Rolf Peschel. He was a German police officer who was shot by his own people because he saved countless Jews and Poles. He was shot for insisting on remaining human.

I talk about my unforgettable friend, a Roman Catholic bishop named Theodor Bensch, who hid several Jews in his chapel and rescued them from deportation to the death camps.

The students' response is always overwhelming. They ask intelligent questions, then some form a line to shake my hand and to embrace me. A few have held me close for many seconds with tears in their eyes. They thanked me for sharing my experiences and volunteered to work for me. Their open affection has touched me to the core of my being. Each time I felt as if they were caressing my heart in which a wound had been festering since the moment my little son was killed. The wound has never healed. These students give me the love my Bruno would have given me had he been granted the chance to stay alive.

I believe fate has been kind to me.

KSIĘDZA BISKUPA
TEODORA BENSCHA

Bishop Teodor Bensch who saved the lives of a number of Jews by hiding them in his own chapel. After the liberation he was arrested by the communist authorities. The author succeeded in sending packages to him behind the Iron Curtain during the 1950s.

Parcel No° **606**

20.4.56.

Delivery Note
POTWIERDZENIE ODBIORU

I acknowledge receipt of GIFT-PARCEL containing:
Potwierdzam odbiór PACZKI-DARU zawierającej:

WIE	SZYNKA w puszce	2 lbs.
	RODZYNKI Sultanas	2 lbs.
	MORELE suszone	1 lb.
	FIGI smyrneńskie	½ lb.
	KAWA ziarn., palona	1 lb.
	KAKAO Rowntree	1 lb.
	PIEPRZ, Malabar I	¼ lb.
	HERBATA Liptona	¼ lb.
	czekoladki	½ lb

Signature:
Data i Podpis: *17.5.1956   Ks. Teodor Bensch*

Kindly sign and return in enclosed envelope.
Thank You!

U W A G A :
Prosimy podpisać i koniecznie **odwrotną pocztą** wysłać w załączonej kopercie.

Haskoba Ltd., London S. W. 5., England

Verte!

Parcel No. **3247**

Delivery Note

2.8.56.

By order of:

NES – 6 PUSZEK NESCAFE

*Proszę uprzejmie podziękować nieznanemu ofiarodawcy w moim imieniu.
Ks. T. Bensch*

POTWIERDZENIE ODBIORU

Potwierdzam odbiór w porządku wyżej wymienionej paczki.
I acknowledge receipt of the above parcel in good order.

Signature:
Data i Podpis: *8 wrzesień 1956 r.   Ks. Teodor Bensch*

Kindly sign and return in enclosed envelope. Thank You!

U W A G A :
Prosimy podpisać i koniecznie **odwrotną pocztą** wysłać w załączonej kopercie.

Haskoba Ltd., London S. W. 5., England

Parcel No. **7768**

Delivery Note

29.11.56.

By order of:

MIT w puszkach:
	2 funty	SZYNKI
	1 "	BOCZKU
1 1/2	"	OZORA
	2 "	WIEPRZOWINY
	1 "	MASŁA
	1 "	SMALCU

POTWIERDZENIE ODBIORU

Potwierdzam odbiór w porządku wyżej wymienionej paczki.
I acknowledge receipt of the above parcel in good order.

Signature:
Data i Podpis: *10. I. 1957   Ks. Teodor Bensch*   *Verte!*

Kindly sign and return in enclosed envelope. Thank You!

U W A G A :
Prosimy podpisać i koniecznie **odwrotną pocztą** wysłać w załączonej kopercie.

Haskoba Ltd., London S. W. 5., England

---

*Delivery notes for food packages sent in 1956 to Bishop
Bensch with his signature acknowledging receipt*

Notes in Bishop Bensch's on the reverse of the above. The food packages were sent to him anonymously, so he frequently attached poignant notes asking about the identity of the nameless person who "sends me these packages which sustain my life."

CENTRE D'INFORMATION
DES
ORGANISATIONS INTERNATIONALES CATHOLIQUES

INFORMATION CENTRE
OF THE
INTERNATIONAL CATHOLIC ORGANIZATIONS

CENTRO DE INFORMACIÓN
DE LAS
ORGANIZACIONES INTERNACIONALES CATÓLICAS

GENÈVE (Suisse) October 7th, 1955.
37. Quai Wilson
Tél. 08-05 32 4065

Mrs. Sandra LEVINE
c/o Frau Ablassmayer
Georgenstrasse 79/II
MUNCHEN 13

Dear Mrs. Levine,

                Thanking you for your kind letter of October 4th, I fully appreciate that you don't return to the U.S.A. if you have to be in Geneva for the meeting of the Ministers of Foreign Affairs.

                I would advise you however to obtain information from Rev. Father Kirschke in order to get all facts about the present condition of Msgr. Bishop Bensch, from Obsztyn whom you would like to help. Is he still certainly in USSR or else where ? are any other details available on his present condition ? As you fully realize, these preliminaries are essential before you take any steps.

                With all best wishes
                   sincerely yours,

Letter from the Information Centre of the International Catholic Organizations concerning Bishop Bensch (1955)

* * *

In 1960 my friend Genia Rosenberg lent *I Dared to Live* to Dr. Gideon Hausner, Attorney General of Israel and the prosecutor of the Eichmann Trial. When the book was returned to her she found a letter tucked inside which praised the author. I was happy to learn Hausner was impressed with my work. Since he mentioned that he wanted to meet the author, I called him during my next visit to Israel and he invited me to come to his office.

"I read your book in one session," he said, "and I would like all the young people of Israel to read it. But it must be first translated into Hebrew."

I answered, "I would like that too."

"And," Dr. Hausner continued, "I would like Rolf Peschel, your German friend, to be declared a Righteous Gentile."

I said, "I would like that too."

Dr. Hausner subsequently found a translator and referred me to a publisher. After two years *I Dared to Live* became a best seller in Israel.

Dr. Hausner also sent me to the Yad Vashem Holocaust Museum in Jerusalem. There I was informed about the procedure of honoring Rolf as a Righteous Gentile. I would have to submit an application in which Rolf's good deeds were listed plus the affidavits of at least two witnesses.

I wrote to three people in Warsaw who had been my coworkers at Vinetta and asked them to write everything they knew about Rolf's activities. It took a long time before I received their stories and affidavits. Then, armed with the reports of two more witnesses from New York, I was sure my application to Yad Vashem would yield successful results immediately.

But it wasn't that easy.

The director of the special commission whose job it was to judge who was to be honored as a Righteous Gentile decided that a German in a position to help some Jews could have harmed other Jews.

I was devastated. Rolf harm Jews? The irony was that he had lost his life, had been shot by the Gestapo, because he saved the lives of Jews as well as Poles.

A long struggle to establish Rolf as a Righteous Gentile ensued, and it lasted for ten years. It took up all my time and energy. I could concentrate on nothing else. I stopped writing. I hoped I would live long enough to see the results of my efforts. My friends were sympathetic, but thought it was futile to go on. They pointed out that I had immortalized Rolf's goodness in my book and why pursue it further? But I could not stop. I hired a history professor in Poland (at the time under a communist regime) to go through the war records at the Warsaw Archives. It took him many months. He could find no criticism of Rolf Peschel.

Yad Vashem assigned Michael Gilead, a Holocaust survivor, to research the Rolf Peschel case. He was formerly the chief of the Israeli police and he must have had a passion for truth and justice, for he bought fifteen books and spent two months researching Nazi activities in Poland. He submitted the results of his findings which consisted of seventeen meticulously composed pages to the Commission for the Designation of the Righteous at Yad Vashem.

On the January 23, 1997, the Commission proclaimed Rolf Peschel a Righteous Gentile, acknowledging that as one who saved Jewish lives, he maintained his humane behavior against all odds.

On October 26, 1998, a ceremony took place in Mannheim, Germany, in which Dr. Roland Zieber, Rolf's younger half-brother, received a medal from the Israeli Ambassador to Germany to immortalize Rolf Peschel.

In the Alley of Righteous Gentiles at the Yad Vashem in Jerusalem, a tree was planted with a plaque attached to it. I was overwhelmed and relieved and profoundly grateful to Yad Vashem for letting me express — albeit in a small way — my immense gratitude to Rolf Peschel, not only for saving the lives of others, but for saving my sister's and my own life as well.

Fate was kind to me.

* * *

In 1955 I was shocked to read a news report about Bishop Bensch being arrested in his homeland, Communist Poland. The bishop had saved the lives of several Jews during the war. It occurred to me that now the survivors had the opportunity to help him out. I wanted to look for them. But I had known only one woman and her young niece whom Father Bensch had saved and, unfortunately, I could no longer remember her name. I made up my mind to take it upon myself to help the bishop.

The author with Pope John Paul II

The author with Pope John Paul II

I flew to neutral Switzerland, got in touch with the American Ambassador, Mr. Cowen, and told him my story. He told me the United States did not interfere in the affairs of other countries, and that I should contact the International Catholic Organization in Geneva.

The director of the organization, a woman named De Romer, was very sympathetic. She immediately had a plan. A meeting of foreign ministers was about to take place and I would be given the opportunity to hand an "open letter" to the Russian minister. But first she suggested I fly to Munich, make an appointment with Father Kirschke who headed the Polish desk at Radio Free Europe. He would know more about the problem and would advise me further.

In Munich Father Kirschke said, "The plan is disastrous. The bishop was arrested because he was accused of making contact with the West. An American trying to help the Bishop would only hurt him more."

"But I want to do something for him," I insisted.

"The bishop is under house arrest. The only way you could conceivably help him is to send him packages anonymously from somewhere other than the United States. I can open an account for you in London. As a matter of fact, I do the same thing for my own family."

I agreed at once. From then on, every month a package from London was shipped to the bishop in Warsaw and the shipping company mailed me the bishop's signed receipts.

The bishop died two or three years later, and, a couple of years later, Cardinal Wyszinski was allowed to travel from Poland to visit the Vatican. Father Kirschke went to Rome to meet the Cardinal. There he was informed that Bishop Bensch had said on his death-bed, "If you ever get out of Poland, please find my benefactor and bless him or her." But Father Kirschke was in Germany and I was in America and the blessing never materialized.

Forty-seven years passed, and then something extraordinary happened. Pope John Paul II asked Cardinal Cassidy to arrange a commemoration for the six million Jews murdered by the Nazis during World War Two. The "Holocaust Concert" was scheduled for April 7, 1994.

Survivors from around the world were invited to the Vatican. About one hundred of them came to Rome. Luckily my husband and I were amongst them. We were the only ones from New York.

By six o'clock on the evening of April 7, many thousands of people had bought tickets to attend the concert. We, the survivors, were the guests of honor.

The Pope was sitting on a podium in the center of a vast hall. On one side sat the President of Italy, and on the other, the Chief Rabbi of Italy. The Pope delivered a speech in Italian, then gave a synopsis in English, and finished with a Polish word, "dziekuye" (thank you). Actor Richard Dreyfus recited the Kaddish, the Jewish prayer for the dead. Gilbert Levine conducted the British Royal Orchestra. (A few months later he was knighted by the Pope.)

But it was our individual audience with the Pope which imprinted itself on my heart. At 11.00 a.m. we were moving in single file toward the podium. My friend Julia Schiffer was just ahead of me. When she reached the Pope I heard her say, "Holy Father, antisemitism is on the rise again. Please help us."

The Pope tapped her shoulder and said, "We will fight together!"

"Are you an actress?" the Pope asked me.

"No," I said. Perhaps I should have said that I was a writer. But I was in a daze. I don't remember what else I said except "My father was a Belzer Chassid."

"Yes," the Pope said, "Yes, Belz. . . ."

I have forgotten at which point he put his hands on both my cheeks and kissed the top of my head.

Many survivors were moved to tears. Later, people asked me what I had said that had led the Pope to give me, and only me, this exceptional blessing. I had no answer.

Back in my hotel room I relived my experience. I felt the touch of the Pope's hands on my cheeks. I felt, as if embraced by a soft cloud, his aura of warmth and affection. I saw again his smiling face that radiated such genuine goodness and humility, and I wondered whether he had descended to our level or whether he had lifted us up to his heights. That night, the Pope had created an ambiance of perfect equality.

It now occurs to me I may have the answer to the puzzle of why Pope John Paul had given me such an exceptional blessing. In some mysterious way Bishop Bensch's wish to have me blessed had reached the Pope who, aware or unaware, had fulfilled the wish of dying man.